ACA Simplified

Advanced Level Financial Reporting Exam Room Notes

ICAEW
PARTNER IN
LEARNING

A Reminder About Copyright

Disclaimer

The text in this book does not amount to professional advice on any particular technical matter and should not be taken as such. No reliance should be placed on the content as the basis for any investment or other decision or in connection with any advice given to third parties.

ACA Simplified expressly disclaims all liability for any losses or other claims, whether direct, indirect, incidental, consequential or otherwise arising in relation to the use of these materials.

We have made every effort to ensure that the materials are accurate and free from error. Please inform us immediately if you believe that you have discovered any problems with the text.

Whilst we strongly believe that our learning materials are an effective method of preparing for your examinations, ACA Simplified does not accept any liability whatsoever for your ultimate performance in the examination as a result of using this text.

Other ACA Simplified Resources for CR and SBM (and a discount!)

In addition to this book, we provide a range of other study resources for CR and SBM.

On-Demand Video Tuition

Our popular on-demand video courses provide a convenient way to obtain expert tutor guidance for CR and SBM. Our courses can be viewed at any time and as often as you wish – perfect for revising the tricky technical areas of the syllabus!

Our courses contain advice on examination technique, planning methods and time management. We also provide a large number of Tutor Talkthroughs of past paper, Question Bank and ICAEW Mock questions, helping you to identify the patterns in terms of what is rewarded in the model answer each time a topic is tested. This method of reviewing model answers in "batches" of examples on the same topic can be very effective as it teaches you what the examiners are going to be looking for every time. We also review the mark allocation in past paper answers so that you can understand how to allocate your time effectively.

As a thank you for purchasing this book, we are pleased to offer you a **10% discount on the 2018 edition of our CR or SBM on-demand courses (or both!)**. Simply email us with your proof of purchase for this book and we will send you a discount code to obtain your 10% discount. This offer is only available if you contact us **before** purchasing your on-demand course(s): retrospective discounts will not be provided. Your discount request must be received no later than 30 June 2018 (in respect of the July 2018 sitting) and no later than 15 October 2018 (in respect of the November 2018 sitting). This offer is limited to one discount per course per original purchaser of this book: no discount will be provided on any second-hand purchase of the book. No cash alternative will be provided. This offer is not available to students on our classroom CR or SBM tuition courses and not to any students whose access to our on-demand courses is paid for by their employer. Please allow 5 working days for your unique access code to be sent by email. All other aspects of the discount are subject to our reasonable discretion and the offer may be withdrawn at any time without notice.

For further information on our on-demand courses, including a free video explanation of how the courses work, please see our website at **www.acasimplified.com**.

Further Study Books and Exam Room Notes

We produce interactive, self-test Q&A books for Advanced Level Financial Reporting and Advanced Level Audit and Assurance. We have condensed and simplified the syllabus content into hundreds of short-form questions that help you learn by testing yourself – much more effective than trying to learn simply by reading from the page or making notes. Our Q&As provide an ideal way to build your technical knowledge so that you can then attempt full exam-standard questions on the basis of a firmer foundation of understanding.

In addition to this set of Exam Room Notes for Financial Reporting, we provide a set of Exam Room Notes covering Audit & Assurance for the Advanced Level. This set of Exam Room Notes covers not only audit risks & procedures but also provides quick reference notes on specialist assurance areas such as Corporate Governance, internal auditing, social and environmental auditing, and so on. Our Audit & Assurance Exam Room Notes therefore provide you with coverage for all types of audit and assurance question in both CR and SBM.

Our Strategic Business Management Exam Room Notes provide reminder notes on over 100 key SBM topics such as acquisitions, valuations, strategic models, Big Data, business development, ethics for SBM and other areas.

Please note that whilst our Strategic Business Management Exam Room Notes do contain summaries of the financial reporting areas tested in recent SBM examinations, we would recommend that you take this set of Advanced Level Financial Reporting Exam Room Notes into your SBM examination (even if you also purchase our Strategic Business Management Exam Room Notes) as this will provide the maximum possible coverage of the different FR areas that could be tested.

Our Strategic Business Management Exam Room Notes are the only set of Advanced Level Exam Room Notes which are specific to a particular Advanced Level paper – our other 2 sets of Advanced Level Exam Room Notes (Advanced Level Audit & Assurance Exam Room Notes and Advanced Level Financial Reporting Exam Room Notes) are useful for **both** CR and SBM.

For further information on these resources, please see our website at **www.acasimplified.com**.

How to Use this Book and Revision Advice

Thank you for purchasing this set of *Advanced Level Financial Reporting Exam Room Notes 2018*. We have reviewed and fully updated the 2017 edition of the book in light of the new 2018 Corporate Reporting syllabus.

We have carefully summarised and simplified the complex ACA Financial Reporting syllabus (both Advanced Level and Professional Level) into **80** key topic areas. We have arranged these topics **alphabetically** for ease of reference: we believe that this is a more sensible presentation than organising the topics by Study Manual chapter (particularly as our content is derived from the Study Manuals for both Corporate Reporting and Financial Accounting and Reporting!) – using our presentation, you can skip straight to the topic without having to remember which chapter of the Study Manuals (or related notes) to check.

We present a complete **alphabetical list of topics starting on page 15**. If you know what topic you need to check, then use this list to quickly find the correct page. Alternatively, simply flick through the book looking at the headings in the top right of the page to find the topic.

We would emphasise that our notes are merely intended to be memory joggers to be used in the exam – you must also invest some time in learning the relevant principles and practising full questions: you will not pass simply from using this book with no other preparation and you must get some experience of using the book in practice exams so that you understand (1) what information is available in the book and (2) where to find it quickly.

We also strongly recommend that you highlight the points which are important to you – we have tried to prepare full and thorough notes to cover all exam-relevant aspects in each topic but everyone is different and so you will need to work out what is most useful to you personally.

Without this careful practice and familiarisation, you will spend too long looking around in the book for information when really in the examination you need to be working as quickly as possible and simply using the book as a memory jogger of content that you have learnt well already. **The more you use the book before the examination, the more quickly you will be able to work** – working quickly is absolutely vital for your examination and you must at all costs avoid spending too long looking points up.

Where possible, we include a **suggested mark allocation for a topic** (assuming that the topic is examined in the **FR-focused** CR question: normally Q2 in CR) to give you some guidance as to how much time to spend on a particular topic. The suggested mark allocation is based on our review of past paper markschemes, as well as our judgement and experience, including our experience of teaching the old Business Reporting paper on which Corporate Reporting is heavily based. However, **always use your own judgement to determine the number of marks**, looking firstly at the amount of Exhibit material relating to the issue (the more material, the more marks) and also looking at the other topics tested, before deciding on your mark and time allocation.

For some topics which have not been examined to date we have not included a suggested mark allocation as this would not be based on any hard data and could be misleading. Therefore, the fact that a particular topic does not state a suggested mark allocation is not an error or omission in the book.

Please note that, as indicated, the suggested mark allocation assumes that you are attempting the **FR-focused CR question** (normally Q2 in CR). You should reduce the mark allocation to perhaps 2/3 of the estimate stated when you are attempting the audit-focused or mixed audit & FR questions (normally Q1 and Q3, respectively, in CR) as the markscheme will have to make room for auditing marks – the markscheme is designed to prevent you passing simply because you are very good at only **one** of the skills of FR **or** auditing. Therefore, if you are strong at FR please do not try to do too much FR in the audit-focused or mixed audit & FR question.

We strongly recommend that you use the book in all revision and practice mock attempts from now on – otherwise you will not learn where to find the necessary information under time pressure.

How to Not Use this Book

Please do not try to use this book in the examination without first spending some time getting used to where to find relevant information. It is not possible simply to turn up on exam day and expect to pass by using this book – rather, you must prepare fully before the examination by practising plenty of questions and reading the Study Manual. This book will simply provide you with **reminders** of content that you should already know – it will not provide you with everything you need to know on a topic that you have not properly studied already.

We have tried to organise the notes in s user-friendly manner, using an alphabetical approach as far as possible. However, there is no substitute for actively using the book during your practice attempts, allowing you to understand and highlight the priority reminder areas for you personally, as this will ensure that you know where to locate the necessary information.

Inline Definition Concept – The Importance of Avoiding a Generic Answer

We have tried to produce a detailed and thorough set of notes which focuses on key definitional and technical issues. This should give you all the gener**al** reminders that you need but in order to prevent your answer therefore becoming gene**ric** in nature it is important that you apply the **general** points to the **specific** data and scenario given. You must definitely avoid a "listing out" approach where you simply copy out the IFRS standards – anyone can copy out material so this is not what the examiners want to see.

Rather than first copying out the IFRS rules and only then going on to refer to the data/Exhibit (or running out of time to properly use the data because you have spent too long writing out the IFRS rules), we strongly recommend that you work the other way around and use what we call "inline definition". This means that you first identify and quote something relevant from the data/Exhibit and only then refer to the IFRS rule/definition in the second part of the sentence (but all in the same line of writing). This will prevent you copying out generic content at the start of your answer which you go on to repeat anyway when you apply the rules to the data.

As an example, rather than simply writing out the 3 criteria for a provision to be recognised before then looking at the data, start with the data and state if this indicates whether 1 or more of the criteria are satisfied. For example, you could say that "The conclusion of the legal case creates a 'past obligating event' and the entity's legal team is confident that the figure of £2m is a 'reliable estimate' of a 'probable outflow of economic resources'". This sentence **both defines and applies in the same line** so it is a much more efficient use of time than copying out definitions and only then moving to the application section (in practice, we know that many students who have an inefficient writing style often do not even get to the application section in some parts of the answer, leaving them only with some copied out definitional points which will not really score very well).

Forex Consolidation – The Importance of Taking in a Worked Example

We have provided detailed reminder notes on how to consolidate a foreign subsidiary into the group accounts in our section starting on page 84. Hopefully these notes will help you understand the process. However, given the complexity of forex consolidation and the fact that this topic has not been tested as an entire question yet in CR, we would strongly recommend that you find a reasonably detailed example of a forex consolidation from a recent past paper or the Question Bank and take an annotated version of this into the examination with you. Together with the reminders in this book, this combination should give you a good chance of performing well in this tricky topic which was occasionally the basis of an entire financial reporting question under the predecessor Business Reporting paper.

In respect of all other topics, we believe that the notes provided here should be sufficient in themselves – however, as advised above, you are strongly recommended to practise a number of questions whilst using this book as this practice will reveal whether you feel you need any additional pro formas or notes. We have tried to be thorough but everyone will have their own strengths and weaknesses.

Some General Tips Regarding Revision for the Advanced Level

We strongly recommend that you do as many practice questions from the relevant Study Manual (whether CR or SBM) and do not rely simply on the Question Bank. We know that the instinct of many students is to go straight to the Question Bank but in both CR and SBM we have seen several past paper questions where the content is closer to that within the Study Manual than it is to anything contained in any Question Bank questions. We think it is quite likely that the examiners will have the Study Manual open and in front of them when they are setting questions to ensure that the questions are fair and only cover content within the Study Manual: compared to this resource, the Question Bank is less relevant. Whilst we recognise there are a large number of questions in the Study Manual (particularly for CR), we do believe that this will be time well spent.

We strongly recommend that you build some time into your revision plan to review your FAR and A&A notes. We also recommend that you allocate some study time to practise past papers from both of these subjects. This is because a large number of marks at the Advanced Level will be based on brought forward knowledge rather than the content of the Advanced Level study materials. The examiners frequently comment that the level of brought forward knowledge is poor (particularly in relation to Groups) so they are likely to continue to test this knowledge and, after all, the Advanced Level is the last opportunity for the examiners to test your professional competence as a Chartered Accountant – you should still be able to explain the IFRS treatment of brought forward topics, as well as to advise on audit risks and procedures, if you are to go on and practise as a Chartered Accountant.

We are aware that many students tend to focus on the new Advanced Level study materials and this is completely understandable because there is a lot to learn and some areas such as forex consolidation and Deferred Tax are quite complicated. However, you should be aware that in many Advanced Level papers **over half of the marks available are actually for brought forward topics**. For this reason, we have reviewed the FAR syllabus in detail and have also analysed FAR past papers and mocks when preparing this set of Advanced Level Financial Reporting Exam Room Notes. Hopefully this will give you some useful reminders but obviously it will be best if you have also revised your brought forward knowledge yourself.

In addition to this set of Advanced Level Financial Reporting Exam Room Notes, we do have a number of other resources available to help you with the Advanced Level:

Advanced Level Audit Q&A 2018 – hundreds of short form practice questions to learn the Audit syllabus in an active way

Advanced Level Financial Reporting Q&A 2018 – hundreds of short form practice questions to learn the Financial Reporting syllabus in an active way

Advanced Level Audit & Assurance Exam Room Notes 2018 – very similar to this book but obviously relating to the important area of audit risks & procedures and also specialist assurance topics

Strategic Business Management Exam Room Notes 2018 – again very similar to this book but covering all key SBM numerical and narrative areas

Smashing Strategic Business Management 2018 – our student-focused and practical guide to planning and revising for the SBM examination, including explanation of our unique MAP planning strategy, revision of key assurance, business strategy and financial management areas and detailed discussion of writing style and ethics for SBM.

Please see our website at **www.acasimplified.com** for further details on the above texts.

As a large number of Advanced Level marks will be available for brought forward knowledge, you may also be interested in our set of Professional Level materials – to assist with your revision, we would particularly recommend our Audit & Assurance Q&A 2018 and Financial Accounting & Reporting Q&A 2018 for CR and our Business Strategy Q&A 2018 and Financial Management Q&A 2018 for SBM.

Changes to the Advanced Level Financial Reporting Syllabus for Examinations in 2018

The updates to create the 2018 syllabus for the financial reporting elements of the Advanced Level are fortunately very minor indeed, and significantly less extensive than the updates made in the prior year to create the 2017 syllabus. This is therefore good news if you started to study the Advanced Level in 2017 as there are not many new points to learn. It also means that ICAEW past papers and Mocks for previous examination sittings should generally remain valid as sources of practice.

We have set out below the changes that we have identified in the 2018 edition of the Corporate Reporting Study Manual. As the Strategic Business Management Study Manual contains condensed versions of the same financial reporting rules set out in the Corporate Reporting Study Manual, we have only analysed the changes in the Corporate Reporting Study Manual below.

Before reviewing the specific changes, we would like to make you aware that we have noted several instances which suggest that the new, incoming financial reporting standards such as IFRS 9, IFRS 14, IFRS 15 and IFRS 17 are more likely to be tested in 2018: the examiners have subtly changed the relevant text in the Study Manual from the previous statement in the 2017 edition that the relevant standard is "not examinable but an area which you should have an awareness of" to a statement in the 2018 edition that now indicates that you "may be examined" on forthcoming changes in the relevant IFRS. Please see below for further details on these subtle changes in wording which we think you should be aware of. Fortunately, the Study Manual has not added much new content on these areas, which remain largely narrative in nature without any numerical worked examples available so you should be able to obtain the marks relatively easily. We have updated the 2018 edition of this book to include a bit more narrative detail on the relevant areas even though, as just mentioned, there have not been many additions to the syllabus content on these new standards compared to the 2017 syllabus: the main change in 2018 is rather in relation to the wording on the extent to which you might be tested on the relevant area.

As these standards are topics which are primarily answered in a narrative manner, it is important that you resist the temptation to list out too many notes as there are not likely to be all that many marks available.

Although we have indicated that the areas are now more examinable, please do not go to the other extreme and spend all your time writing out notes if the relevant topics are tested: we simply mean that you are more likely to be examined on these areas than in prior years, not that the focus of the whole examination has now shifted as the markscheme will allocate almost all of the marks to discussion of the extant standards.

Based on our review, there have been no changes at all to the CR Study Manual in relation to the chapters on earnings per share, reporting of non-financial liabilities, employee benefits, share-based payment and foreign currency translation and hyperinflation. In most other cases, as indicated below, the changes are very minor in nature.

We will now provide a listing of the changes which we have identified, including a page reference to the 2018 edition of the Study Manual and, where possible, a corresponding reference to the relevant page in the 2017 edition.

p440 (2017 edition: p432)

The first 3 Learning objectives at the top of this page are new. However, the new Learning objectives, in our opinion, simply explicitly state certain objectives which have always been relevant to the Advanced Level.

p446 (2017 edition: p438)

The first paragraph at the top of this page is new. Also, Section 1.5.1 on the "Draft Practice Statement" in relation to the application of materiality to financial statements is new.

p498 (2017 edition: p490)

The first Learning objective at the top of this page is new. Again, in our opinion, this new Learning objective is simply an explicit statement of objective which has always been relevant to the Advanced Level.

p580 (2017 edition: p570)

The first Learning objective at the top of this page has been slightly amended to explicitly state that candidates need to be able to "explain the role of data analytics in financial asset and liability valuation". Data analytics and Big Data issues are currently a very important theme in the ACA with syllabus content being added to almost all ACA papers on these topics over the last couple of years. We would always advise students to ensure they are fully aware of syllabus content in relation to these "trendy" topics within accountancy.

p605 to p606 (not in the 2017 edition)

Section 5.5 on "Current developments in relation to IFRS 17" is new.

p678 (2017 edition: p666 for first point – second point is not in the 2017 edition)

The paragraph under the heading for Section 4.2 has been amended to say that candidates may now be "examined" on how IFRS 16 could affect future accounting periods. The previous edition stated that IFRS 16 "is not examinable" and that candidates only need to be "aware of it as a current issue or when considering how future accounting periods may be affected". There is therefore now a more explicit statement in the 2018 edition that you may be "examined" on IFRS 16.

Additionally, the 2 "Definitions" and the Sections on "Control" and "Non-lease components" on this page are also new. Similarly, the Worked example at the bottom of p678 is new.

p679 (not in the 2017 edition)

The Interactive question at the bottom of the page is new.

p680 (2017 edition: p666 to p667)

Further text on how to treat a sale and leaseback under IFRS 16 has been added on this page. Text has also been added to state that "a knowledge of IFRS 9, IFRS 15 and IFRS 16 is required and may be examinable" even though there are other extant standards in these areas.

Section 4.2.8 on Transition is new.

Interactive question 8 on Sale and leaseback is new and replaces an Interactive question in the previous edition on Problems with lease accounting. We would note that the new Interactive question is more numerical in nature than the question which has now been removed.

Overall, based on the changes to p678, p679 and p680 which we have reviewed here, there does seem to be an indication that a better level of knowledge of IFRS 16 is now required and that the area may be more examinable than in the prior year.

p686 (2017 edition: p673)

Text has been added to clarify that the audit tests on this page are relevant to IAS 17 but there have been no changes to the tests themselves.

p710 (2017 edition: p698)

The final Learning objective is new. However, in our opinion, this Learning objective is simply an explicit statement of an objective which has always been applicable at the Advanced Level.

p712 to p713 (2017 edition: p700)

Text has been added to Section 1.2.1. The new text starts at the second paragraph of Section 1.2.1 ("A contract is not an equity instrument …") and ends at the top of p713 (" … only in the event of liquidation of the issuer.").

The 2 Worked examples on p713 are both new.

p768 to p770 (not in the 2017 edition)

Section 4 on Application of IFRS 13 to financial instruments is new but mostly contains syllabus content which is also in Chapter 2 of the 2018 Study Manual and which was also in the same Chapter in the 2017 Study Manual. Therefore, despite this new Section on IFRS 13, there have not been any substantial additions to the Study Manual. We recommend that you look at the new Worked example and Interactive question on p769 as these are both useful questions to practise.

p779 (2017 edition: p765)

The text under Section 6.10 has been amended. In the previous edition, the text stated that IFRS 9 "is not yet examinable in detail, so you need to know the current rules under IAS 39". The 2018 Study Manual now states that "While IAS 39 remains the extant standard, some knowledge of IFRS 9 is required, and it may be examinable."

p780 (2017 edition: p765)

The amendment here is very similar to the amendment reviewed above in relation to p779: the text is now more explicit that IFRS 9 "may be examinable".

p786 (not in the 2017 edition)

Section 7.15.5 on "IFRS 9 financial asset classification and impairment" is new.

p787 (not in the 2017 edition)

Section 7.15.6 on "Loan commitments and financial guarantee contracts" is new.

p792 (2017 edition: p776)

The final paragraph on this page has been slightly amended from the prior edition to explain that IFRS 9 requires a principles-based approach to hedge accounting and the alignment of accounting with risk management activities. The amended paragraph then explains that the IFRS 9 approach to hedge accounting is now covered in Chapter 17 of the Study Manual.

A substantial amount of content that used to be included on p776 to p778 of the 2017 Study Manual has been deleted from the corresponding part of the 2018 Study Manual and moved into Chapter 17 of the 2018 edition. Please see our further points on this process below.

p831 to p833 (not in the 2017 edition)

The Worked example on a "Fixed rate loan" is new.

p833 (not in the 2017 edition)

Section 4.2.1 on Interest rate futures and the related Worked example are both new.

p849 to p854 (2017 edition: p776 to p778, plus new content)

Section 9 on "Current developments: IFRS 9 changes" is new and expands a similar section previously on p833 of the 2017 Study Manual. Content which used to be included on p776 to p778 of the 2017 Study Manual has also been moved into this new section.

p1066 (2017 edition: p1044)

The final paragraph on this page is new.

p1195 (2017 edition: p1173)

There have been minor changes to Section 6.2.4 to allow for the fact that the Exposure Draft referred to in the 2017 Study Manual is now classified as an "amendment" to the rules in the 2018 Study Manual. The first sentence of Section 6.2.4 therefore now refers to an "amendment" that was issued in January 2016 (rather than to an Exposure Draft issued in 2014 as in the previous edition of the Study Manual). The final paragraph of the same Section is now significantly shorter and explains that the "amendment" is effective from January 2017, replacing a more substantial discussion of Exposure Draft points in the previous edition. A numerical Worked Example in relation to this "amendment" is then provided on pages 1195 and 1196: we recommend that you look at this question. We have incorporated relevant notes into the 2018 edition of this book.

Finally, in addition to our review of changes in relation to financial reporting rules, please note that p1334 to p1338 of the 2018 Study Manual are new because Section 9 on "Data and analysis" has been added. This Section provides some useful advice on how to analyse financial data, including a Worked example to practice so although these pages do not, strictly speaking, relate to financial reporting, we highlight the addition here.

Sources Used

To develop this book, we have reviewed the following sources for indicators of key points which the examiners want to see in your answers:

CR past papers (covering the period from launch of the CR paper in July 2014 to the latest available model answers for the November 2017 examination)

CR ICAEW mock exams (2 papers per sitting covering the period from launch of the CR paper in July 2014 to the latest available model answers for the November 2017 mocks)

CR ICAEW Question Bank 2018 (covering all questions in the Question Bank)

FAR past papers (covering the period from launch of the FAR paper in September 2013 to the latest available model answers for the December 2017 examination)

FAR ICAEW mock exams (2 papers per sitting covering the period from launch of the FAR paper in September 2013 to the latest available model answers for the December 2017 mocks)

We have reviewed FAR materials because the examiners will most certainly test brought forward Professional Level knowledge at the Advanced Level – please do not fall into the classic mistake of concentrating too much on Advanced Level knowledge: **most of the marks for financial reporting in a typical CR paper will actually be based on brought forward topics**. (Please see the above section on general tips for more on this point.)

In cases where a topic has not been examined to date but has a substantial Study Manual section dedicated to it (for example, Agriculture or Regulatory Deferral Accounts) we have summarised the relevant Study Manual section as there is no past paper or mock exam content to consider. **However, this is very much the exception and we have, wherever possible, relied on past paper, mock or Question Bank model answers in order to ensure that we have focused on points that are more likely to rewarded.**

Disclaimers

This book has been developed by reviewing official ICAEW materials such as the Study Manual, Question Bank, past papers and mock examinations. In preparing the book, we have assumed that these materials are correct unless a relevant errata sheet has been issued by ICAEW. Given the time constraints to produce the book, we have not checked every single technical point back to the underlying IFRS rules and have instead **assumed that the ICAEW materials are correct**. We cannot be held responsible for any errors in the underlying ICAEW material which had not been notified to tutor companies before the time of finalisation of the script of the book (early March 2018).

We have developed this book by working backwards from common themes in model answers to identify the core areas that you need to cover to ensure a passing grade – our aim has not been to summarise every page of the relevant Study Manuals (both Professional and Advanced Level) nor to try to cover every possible way in which topics **could** be tested: if we tried to do this, we would end up with a book the same length as the Study Manuals and therefore not suitable as a **quick reference resource** in the examination. Our aim has been to create an "exam focused" text i.e. one that responds to the most commonly tested areas and highlights the most common student errors when attempting to answer these areas rather than as any kind of replacement for proper study of the Study Manual. **Many of the changes made to create the 2018 syllabus appear to us to be highly technical in nature and only relevant in very specific scenarios so we have not added every additional 2018 syllabus point into this book.**

We have also concentrated on those points contained in model answers as sometimes valid points contained in the Study Manuals do not appear to be given credit and therefore you would be wasting time to include these points (even if they are completed correct from a technical point of view). No book of the type we have tried to write here can cover every possible matter that could be tested from a combination of 2 different ACA papers (FAR and CR) and there is a **very significant risk** of running out of time if you go into matters in too much detail so we have purposefully not tried to cover everything.

In any examination, you will need to apply your general understanding to the specific scenario set and we cannot anticipate exactly what will be required. Therefore, we do not make any claim that this book covers all potential examination points – it has instead been designed to help you with the **more commonly assessed points**. We therefore cannot accept any complaints that the book did not cover every single issue tested in your own particular examination as the book is instead designed to help you ensure a good performance in the **more commonly tested areas** which should almost certainly constitute more than enough marks to obtain a passing grade in any CR examination.

Finally, please note that all examiners' reports for the Advanced Level examinations complain about candidates using "**generic**" points in their answers – this is a particular problem at the Advanced Level because students are able to refer extensively to their own notes in these "open book" examinations. The points that we have included in these notes are simply meant to **remind** you of technical content that you should already know and we **very strongly recommend against simply copying out the points made in this book** – many of these may not be relevant to your specific question and you must in any case show the examiner that you have responded to the data given in your question – **anyone can copy out notes and you will not be rewarded for doing so**.

Thank you for reading these disclaimers and we hope this section has made it clearer to you how the book should (and should not) be used.

A Reminder About Copyright

Please do not photocopy or otherwise distribute this book, either in whole or part. Copyright theft is a crime and we will pursue individuals who infringe our copyright.

Copyright theft is a clear breach of professional ethics and may therefore be reported to the ICAEW.

We have put a considerable amount of time and effort into developing innovative materials which we genuinely feel will give you an edge in the exams. We would be grateful if you would respect these efforts by not copying this text.

Thank you again for your purchase and we hope you find the book useful. Please do let us have your feedback at **getqualified@acasimplified.com**.

List of Acronyms

CSFP	Consolidated Statement of Financial Position
CSoCIE	Consolidated Statement of Changes in Equity
CSPL	Consolidated Statement of Profit or Loss
NCI	Non-Controlling Interest
P&L	Profit or Loss account
SCF	Statement of Cash Flows
SFP	Statement of Financial Position
SoCIE	Statement of Changes in Equity

Table of Contents

General Tips for Answering CR Questions

Use the scenario!

Anyone can copy out standards from notes or the IFRS book – only a good candidate can apply their knowledge to the **unique aspects of the scenario set**.

Make sure your answer is scenario-specific by referring extensively to key **facts and figures** stated in the scenario Exhibits – avoid a "**listing out**" approach.

Inline definition

Relatedly, rather than copying out a standard at the start of the question, try to start your sentences with key facts and figures from the scenario and only **then** mention the relevant IFRS rules **as you go along** (in the **second part** of each sentence).

This way you will show that you know the rules but you will be guaranteeing that you are **also** using the **data** because you are starting your points with Exhibit information which could not have been pre-prepared.

Journals – check what you are being asked to do (journals from scratch or adjusting journals)

Always read the question wording carefully to check whether you need to incrementally **adjust** any entries **already made** or whether the journal is required from scratch (i.e. no entry at all has been made by the client) – the examiners have stated that students often assume that no entries have been made but in practice it is very common to require only a **correcting** journal to what the client has already mistakenly done.

Note that what the client accountant has already done will **very often be wrong** …

Do not forget the NCI (and do not be afraid of him!)

For some reason we find that students are very reluctant to mention the impact of their adjustments/treatment on the NCI in group questions. This is simply a matter of multiplying the adjustment/treatment by a percentage figure (reflecting the NCI holding) so is a very easy way of generating some more marks. The marking will work on a follow through basis so you can still get all the NCI marks even if your underlying approach is wrong.

So as soon as you see that you are attempting a group scenario then make a note somewhere to mention the NCI impact.

Ratios – do not go nuts!

If you enjoy the numbers side of accounting, do not go too crazy with the number of performance ratios and metrics which you calculate – you could calculate figures all day but the point is to state the **key points** in a short space of time.

The official Question Bank contains several questions with 25+ marks for performance review work – note that the real exam papers have thus far allocated **far fewer marks** for performance review as there are also other elements of the question to address.

Therefore do not spend too long on the performance review just because it is relatively straightforward.

Think which question you are attempting

If you are doing the FR-heavy question (generally Q2 in the recent CR examinations) then you will need to go into reasonable **depth** and look at **both** the numbers and narrative aspects to score well. However, if you are attacking exactly the same topic in the other questions (audit-focused and mixed audit & FR) then bear in mind that the number of marks available for any given Financial Reporting topic will be **lower**. Hence just be careful to make your answer a little shorter as otherwise you will spend too long on an issue that is necessarily worth fewer marks simply because it is not being tested in the FR-heavy question.

It is for this reason that our mark allocation estimates are based on assuming that the topic is being tested in an FR-heavy question – ensure that you reduce your mark estimate and related time allocation accordingly if you are not attempting the FR-heavy question.

Am I secretly not very good at Audit?

If you are not an auditor in your day to day work then please ensure that you do write enough for the audit sections of the paper – it is not possible to pass the exam just from great FR work so do not try to hide behind this ability. You must confront your weaker skill and allow enough time to get a good number of audit marks or you will not get the total number of marks needed.

Do not go straight for the calculations

There are indeed specific marks for getting the calculations correct – but the number of marks is nowhere near as many as you may expect. In fact, there will be a lot of marks (and often the **majority** of the marks available) for narrative explanation of the principles and use of the scenario data. Do not neglect these marks by spending too long on the calculations.

Equally, remember that the marking is done on a full follow-through approach so even if your figures are wrong but are correctly discussed then you can still pick up a good number of marks … but only if you leave yourself enough time for writing by not spending too long on the calculations.

Adjustments to the financial statements/Schedule of Uncorrected Misstatements

Often the question will ask you either to process your suggested changes and show how the financial statements would be affected or, in an audit question, to produce a Schedule of Uncorrected Misstatements that shows a 4 column presentation of the Dr and Cr adjustments needed regarding both the Income Statement and the Statement of Financial Position.

These adjustments/schedules are marked on a full follow through approach so you have a chance of scoring all the marks if you simply attempt the section and pull through your figures. There tend to be around 6 marks for doing so, which is relatively generous when everything is based on a follow through approach so **please leave enough time to give this section a good attempt**.

You may wish to set up the adjustments/schedule and add points as you go along when answering the other parts of the question, rather than leaving this as a separate task – at least this way you will definitely start getting **some** of the marks from the adjustments/schedule part of the markscheme whereas if you do not make a start on this part of the answer until you have first dealt with all the issues then there is a chance you might never get started and all those easy, follow through marks will be lost instantly …

Audit procedures – put lots in! And don't just say "Check payables" or similar!

The examiners want to see a large number of procedures mentioned, across a range of risk areas – we would aim for at least 4 different tests per risk area and try to mix these tests up so that you are not just recycling the same test each time.

We do not recommend use of the term "check" in relation to any audit tests – obviously auditing involves the "checking" of information so do not expect any marks to be available for stating such a truism. Additionally, the point of the marks for audit tests and procedures is to spell out exactly **how** the auditor will check information so simply saying "check" does not really answer the question at all.

Accounting Policies, Changes in Accounting Estimates and Errors

The rules here are governed by IAS 8

Accounting policies should be applied consistently for similar transactions, events and conditions

Changes in accounting policy should be rare and should only be made if required by an IFRS or if the change will result in the provision of more reliable and relevant information about the effect of transactions, events or conditions on the entity's position, performance or cash flows

Events which do not constitute a change in accounting policy

Adopting an accounting policy for a **new type** of transaction or event not dealt with previously by the entity

Adopting a **new** accounting policy for a transaction or event which has **not occurred in the past** or which was not material

A decision to adopt a policy of **revaluation** under IAS 16 is not treated as a change of accounting policy under IAS 8

Changes in accounting policy

Such a change must be applied **retrospectively** by adjusting the opening balance of retained earnings

Comparative information should be **restated** unless it is **impracticable** to do so – all comparative information is restated as if the new policy had **always been in force**

In the case of voluntary changes, the nature of the change, reasons for the change (why more reliable and relevant), amount of adjustments and the fact that comparative information has been restated (or that it is impracticable to do so) should be disclosed

Changes in accounting estimates

Such changes must be recognised **prospectively** only

These changes result from new information or new developments and are not corrections of errors

Examples – bad debt (receivables) allowances, useful lives of depreciable assets, adjustments for obsolescence of inventory

Where a change in accounting estimate has a **material** effect in the current period there should be **disclosure** of the **nature** of the change in the accounting estimate and the amount of change (or disclosure of the fact that it is impractical to estimate this)

Cases of doubt

If there is **doubt** as to which type of change it is, IAS 8 requires the change to be treated as a change in accounting **estimate**

Prior period errors

If **immaterial**, these can be corrected through net profit or loss for the **current** period

If **material**, prior period errors should be corrected **retrospectively** – this means there must be recognition, measurement and disclosure of amounts as if the prior period error had never occurred (restating the comparative amounts or, if that is not possible, the opening balances for the earliest prior period presented)

There should be disclosure of the nature of the prior period error, the amount of the correction for each financial statement line item affected, the amount of the correction at the start of the earliest prior period presented and, if retrospective restatement is impracticable, the circumstances which have caused this impossibility and a description of how and from when the error has been corrected

Agriculture

IAS 41 applies permanently to **biological** assets – however, it only applies to **agricultural produce** up to the point of harvest (after this point IAS 2 Inventories applies)

Characteristics of agricultural activities

Capacity to change – a seed grows into a tree; a lamb grows into a sheep

Management of change – reliant on some form of management input for survival

Measurement of change – quality and quantity can both change

Note – ocean fishing is not an agricultural activity as there is no management intervention for the fish to grow: this just happens naturally

Bearer biological assets

These are plant-based biological assets such as grape vines, rubber trees and oil palms

These plants grow crops over several periods and are not themselves consumed – when they are no longer productive they are usually scrapped

These plants should be accounted for under IAS 16 (including the option to use the revaluation model) as they are not directly subject to IAS 41 because they do not have a fair value **themselves** – rather the value is in what they **produce**

The produce of these assets continues to be recognised under IAS 41

Recognition of biological or agricultural assets

Entity **controls** the asset as a result of past events

Probable flow of future economic **benefits** to the entity

FV or cost can be **measured reliably**

Measurement of biological assets

Measure at FV less estimated CTS

CTS do not include any costs to get the product to market such as transport – these should instead be deducted when arriving at FV

> CTS could include auctioneer's commission, government levies, broker commission, transfer taxes and duties

FV should be based on an active quoted market price or if this does not exist then it should be based on a similar recent transaction, similar market prices or sector benchmarks

If FV cannot be determined then recognise at cost less accumulated depreciation and impairment cost – FV should then be used as soon as reliable measurement can be made

Once FV has been used, it is not possible to revert to cost

Measurement of agricultural produce

Measure at FV less estimated costs to sell at the point of harvest

Subsequent measurement is then made by reference to IAS 2

Grouping of assets

It is permissible to group similar assets together if they have consistent attributes throughout the group

If the assets are physically attached to the land then deduct the FV of the land element from the combined FV – land is dealt with under IAS 16 or IAS 40

Gains or losses

Report these directly in profit or loss as they arise

Gains may arise on recognition of a biological asset e.g. birth of a calf

Gains may arise on harvesting as the harvested crop may be worth more than an unharvested crop

Example

An entity owns 10 animals with an average age of 4 years. Halfway through the year it purchases a 4.5 year old animal. FV less estimated CTS were £100 at the start of the year, £120 for a 4.5 year old animal and £140 for a 5 year old animal

Opening value (10 x £100)	1,000
Purchased	120
Change in FV (balancing figure)	**420**
Closing value (11 x £140)	1,540

Disclosures

The entity is encouraged to disclose separately the amount of change in FV less estimated CTS arising from physical changes and price changes

If it is not possible to apply FV and cost is used instead, an explanation should be provided of why it was not possible to establish FV

A full reconciliation of movements in the net cost should be presented with an explanation of the depreciation rate and method used

Assets Held for Sale and Discontinued operations

Suggested mark allocation in an FR question (CR Q2): 5 marks

Key Tips

AHFS and discontinued operations are often both applied to the same scenario – this is often because the entity is classifying an asset as AHFS as a result of ceasing operations in a certain area, which could lead to a discontinued operation

Do not forget to also consider the **discontinued operations** element – many students spot the **AHFS** aspect but not the **discontinued operations** aspects

Linkages – also consider impairment (IAS 36) and provisions (IAS 37)

AHFS criteria

Available for immediate sale in its present condition

Sale highly probable as evidenced by

> active marketing at a price reasonable in relation to the item's fair value
>
> changes to the plan for sale are unlikely
>
> management is committed to the sale
>
> active programme to locate a buyer
>
> sale expected to be completed within 1 year from the date of classification (unless delayed by events or circumstances beyond the entity's control, provided that there is sufficient evidence that the entity is still committed to sell the asset)

If the criteria are met only **after** the reporting date, there should be full **disclosure** in the notes to the financial statements (but the asset should not be treated as AHFS in the current accounting period)

Always consider impairment in AHFS questions

Consider **impairment**, especially if the asset is being sold due to a change in business or market conditions

In other cases, the asset may not meet the AHFS criteria but the change in business situation could mean that the asset is still impaired e.g. if the plant has become "surplus to requirements"

A normal IAS 36 impairment test would then have to be carried out (compare FV less CTS with value in use)

If "surplus to requirements" then value in use will not exceed FV less CTS (because there is no ongoing business value to be obtained from "surplus" equipment) so FV less CTS can be used as the relevant comparator figure

AHFS Treatment – overview

Immediately before classification as held for sale, measure in accordance with the applicable IFRS

On classification as AHFS, measure the asset at the lower of its carrying amount and FV less costs to sell (impairment test)

> If the revaluation model is used, the asset should then be revalued under that model before being classified as AHFS (ignoring the costs to sell for this purpose: only look at FV) but if the cost model is used there should NOT be a revaluation to FV (just a write down to FV less CTS, if lower than carrying amount i.e. no revaluation upwards is possible under the cost model) [see also below]

Charge any impairment loss to profit or loss

Cease depreciation or amortisation

Any subsequent changes in FV less CTS are recognised as a further impairment loss or reversal of an impairment loss – however, reversals cannot exceed cumulative impairment losses to date

Once classified as AHFS the costs to sell should be recognised as part of profit or loss for the period

Reclassify the item as a current asset as its value is expected to be realised within the next 12 months

Asset under the revaluation model meets the AHFS criteria

First measure the asset at the lower of its carrying amount and its FV less costs to sell

Then re-measure the asset to FV (ignoring the costs to sell here) and adjust the revaluation surplus for the gain or loss as required – i.e. revalue the asset at fair value under IAS 16 immediately before the classification as AHFS

Once classified as AHFS the costs to sell should be recognised as part of profit or loss for the period in the normal way

Abandonment of non-current assets

Note that the requirements of IFRS 5 relate to assets classified as AHFS because their carrying amounts will be recovered principally through a **sale transaction**

IFRS 5 does **not** apply to assets that will not be **sold** (e.g. scrapped)

Leave such assets in their existing non-current asset category, continue to recognise depreciation and recognise any profit or loss on abandonment at the time of abandonment rather than at the earlier time of the decision to abandon them

IAS 16, rather than IFRS 5, will apply in this case

Discontinued operations

Separate disclosure in the P&L and OCI of a "discontinued operation" is required when a company discontinues a "component" of its activities

>A "discontinued operation" is a separate major line of business or geographical area of operations, part of a single co-ordinated plan to dispose of the same or a subsidiary acquired exclusively with a view to resale

>A "component" should be a cash generating unit, meaning that it comprises operations and cash flows that can be clearly distinguished operationally, and for financial reporting purposes, from the rest of the entity

A single amount in the P&L containing the post-tax profit or loss of discontinued operations and post-tax gain recognised on the measurement to FV less CTS on related assets should be disclosed – this should then be split into revenue, expenses and pre-tax profit or loss, related income tax expense, gain on re-measurement and its related income tax expense

In the Statement of Cash Flows there should be disclosure of the net cash flows attributable to operating, investing and financing activities of discontinued operations

Withdrawal from a particular market or product area could qualify under IFRS 5 but some judgement will be required, particularly if the entity continues to undertake a similar activity in another part of the business or online

Motives of Management points

Look out for any incentive for management to treat the operations as "discontinued" in the hope of separately disclosing losses to downplay the significance of those losses by achieving a corresponding improvement in performance from (what management claims are) "continuing" operations

Borrowing costs

Suggested mark allocation in an FR question (CR Q2): 4 marks

Definition

Borrowing costs are defined as **interest and other costs** that an entity incurs in connection with the borrowing funds in relation to a **qualifying asset** (an asset that necessarily takes a **substantial period** of time to get ready for its intended use or sale)

Only borrowing costs that are **directly attributable** to the acquisition, construction or production of the qualifying asset should be capitalised

Ideally use the interest rate on a loan **specifically taken out** for the purpose of building the asset but a **weighted average cost** is permissible if funded from general borrowing (excluding any borrowings from this calculation if they were taken out to finance a different specific purpose or building)

Qualifying asset

A qualifying asset is an asset that takes a **substantial period of time** to get ready for its intended use or sale

An entity is not required to apply IAS 23 to borrowing costs directly attributable to the acquisition, construction or development of assets which on initial recognition are measured at FV or inventories that are manufactured in large quantities on a repetitive basis even if these take a substantial period of time to get ready for use or sale

Costs to capitalise

Interest expense calculated using the Effective Interest Rate as described in IAS 39

Finance charges in respect of finance leases

However, costs should only relate to borrowing which would have been avoided if the expenditure on the qualifying asset had not been made

If financed out of specific borrowing, using the interest rate applicable to that borrowing

If financed out of general borrowing then use the weighted average cost of that borrowing (excluding borrowings to finance a specific purpose or building)

The amount of borrowing costs capitalised could be **limited** because the **carrying amount of the asset including borrowing costs** should not exceed the asset's **recoverable amount**

Commencement of capitalisation

Capitalisation of borrowing costs should commence when the entity meets all 3 of the following conditions

      it incurs expenditure on the asset

      it incurs borrowing costs

it undertakes activities that are necessary to prepare the asset for its intended use

Activities include construction, drawing up plans, obtaining planning permissions, obtaining permissions from utility providers and obtaining other consents required – simply **holding** an asset for **development** without any associated activities is not enough to qualify for capitalisation

(Make sure you **illustrate** each condition with an **example** from the **exam scenario** at the same time that you define the above points – this is to ensure that you don't write things twice and waste time.)

Cessation of capitalisation

Capitalisation should cease when **substantially all** the activities necessary to get the asset ready for its intended use or sale are complete – minor activities such as decoration to a purchaser's specification do not form part of the substantial activities

Availability for sale is what matters, not the actual use or sale – availability for sale normally depends on the asset being physically complete

Building is constructed in parts – if each part is capable of being used/sold separately whilst other parts continue to be constructed, the cessation of capitalisation of borrowing costs should be assessed on the completion of each part – where no part is capable of being used/sold separately until all other parts have been completed, cessation should take place when the last part is completed

Deduction of investment income

Remember to deduct investment income received on invested funds from the total amount capitalised

Remember to state the amount that can be capitalised net of these funds i.e. actually do the calculation for the client

No depreciation

In the question, the asset is probably not yet complete so no depreciation should be charged as it is not ready for use

Disclosure

Costs which have been capitalised in the current period

Capitalisation rate used to determine the amount of borrowing costs eligible for capitalisation

Judgements required

Substantial period of time to get ready

Borrowing costs which are directly attributable

Activities necessary to prepare the qualifying asset

Substantially all the activities necessary are complete

Cash Flow Statement – Example

We provide an example Cash Flow Statement to provide you with basic reminders of issues to consider and where these should be recognised – other entries are of course possible

Ensure that you have practised the use of T-accounts to determine cash amounts paid or received

Remember to mention precisely **where** items should be disclosed in the Cash Flow Statement to create a well explained contrast with the P&L treatment which will apply an accruals approach (e.g. cash amounts in relation to pensions, finance leases, government grants etc)

Cash flows from operating activities

Cash generated from operations (reconciled in a note – see next page for an example)

Interest paid

Income taxes paid

Net cash from operating activities

Cash flows from investing activities

Purchase of property, plant and equipment

Proceeds from the sale of property, plant and equipment

Interest received

Dividends received

Net cash used in investing activities

Cash flows from financing activities

Proceeds from issue of share capital

Proceeds from issue of long-term borrowings

Dividends paid

Net cash used in financing activities

Net increase in cash and cash equivalents

Cash and cash equivalents at beginning of period

Cash and cash equivalents at end of period

Example of a reconciliation note to find Cash generated from operations

This note provides some examples as reminders – other entries may be possible

Profit before tax	X
Depreciation charges	X
Loss on disposal of non-current assets	X
Interest expense	X
Increase in inventories	(X)
Decrease in receivables	X
Increase in payables	X
Cash generated from operations	**X**

Remember to add back non-cash expenses such as depreciation or a loss on disposal on non-current assets as these expenses do not require **cash** to be paid out

Add back interest expense because this amount is based on an accruals approach rather than the **cash** paid – you will deduct the **cash** paid in relation to interest in the next row of the SCF (see previous page)

For the working capital entries (inventories, receivables and payables) think about whether the movement is **good** or **bad** for the business

> **Inventories** – do we want to build up inventories or do we want to sell items rather than holding them? We want to sell rather than put money into inventories so an **increase** in inventories is **bad** and therefore a **negative** cash flow entry

> **Receivables** – we want receivables to **decline** as this means we are getting more cash in (rather than extending credit to customers via the receivables) so if receivables **increase** this is **bad** and therefore a **negative** cash flow entry

> **Payables** – we want to delay paying suppliers for as long as possible (without upsetting them) so a **decline** in payables would be **bad** and therefore a **negative** cash flow entry as it implies that we are settling bills more quickly

(In reality, we would also need to look at the relative amount of business we are doing to determine whether the movement really is good or bad but the above rules of thumb will always help to determine the correct movement (i.e. whether a positive or negative sign is needed.))

Consolidated Statement of Changes in Equity (CSoCIE)

As student performance on the CSoCIE (and single company SoCIE) tends to be poor (according to examiner comments), we include some notes here – you should also ensure that you can handle the more familiar CSFP and CSPL.

Example CSoCIE (figures are purely illustrative and may not reflect any relevant percentage holdings)

	Share capital	Retained earnings	Revaluation surplus	AFS Reserve	Total	NCI	Total
	Attributable to the owners of Example plc						
b/f at 1 Jan 2016	200,000	500,000	100,000	50,000	850,000	25,000	875,000
Total comprehensive income for the year		200,000		5,000	205,000	5,000	210,000
Added on acquisition in year						2,000	2,000
Dividends		(20,000)			(20,000)	(6,000)	(26,000)
c/f at 31 Dec 2016	200,000	680,000	100,000	55,000	1,035,000	26,000	1,061,000

Other reserves could include Shares to be issued (on acquisition of a subsidiary under an agreement to issue shares in future), share premium or a translation reserve, for example.

NCI

There will **nearly always** be entries for NCI's share of the subsidiary's total comprehensive income for the year and dividends paid/payable

There will **sometimes** be entries for the subsidiary's revaluations of non-current assets

If a partly-owned subsidiary is acquired during the year there will be an entry for NCI added on the acquisition of a subsidiary (and likewise eliminated on any disposal during the year)

NCI brought forward will be the NCI share of the subsidiary's equity brought forward or fair value plus NCI share of the subsidiary's post-acquisition reserves

Retained earnings brought forward

Group reserves brought forward = P's reserves brought forward + P% of subsidiary's post-acquisition reserves brought forward +/- goodwill impairment (to start of the year) and any other adjustments to the opening position

Construction Contracts

Suggested mark allocation in an FR question (CR Q2): 4 to 6 marks (depending on the number of calculations needed)

See the **end** of this section for some pro-forma **calculations** that may be required

Note that **IFRS 15** may change the process applied significantly once it enters into force – you only need an "**awareness**" knowledge of IFRS 15 currently so do not go into too much detail but see page 157 for some notes

Fixed price

Revenue is fixed or determinable at the start of the contract – high degree of certainty

Costs are uncertain

Cost plus

Revenue is based on costs incurred plus an agreed profit margin

Profits should definitely occur but there is less certainty about both revenue and costs

Contract revenue

Contract revenue should be built up over the life of the contract

Variations should only form part of contract revenue when it is probable that they will result in revenue and the amount can be measured reliably

Contract costs

Contract costs include costs directly related to the specific contract and an allocation of costs incurred in contract activity in general

The principles are similar to the variable costs which can be capitalised when plant and equipment is manufactured

Overheads can be allocated on a systematic basis, based on normal levels of activity

Costs such as research costs, general administration costs and selling costs should be recognised as expenses and not as contract costs

Contract negotiation costs

These costs relate to negotiations with public bodies

These should be treated in a similar way to development expenses under IAS 38

> Recognise as an expense up to the time when it first becomes probable that the contract will be won

Negotiation costs subsequent to that time should be included in contract costs

Negotiation costs already expensed cannot subsequently be added to contract costs

Finance costs should be included in contract costs under IAS 23

Assessing stage of completion – the different methods available

Costs incurred as a proportion of total costs of the contract (most common method)

Surveys of work performed, carried out by an independent valuer

Measurement of the proportion physically complete e.g. if a number of buildings need to be constructed

Estimate of outcome is reliable

Fixed price contract – estimate of outcome is reliable if

Total contract revenue can be measured reliably

Probable that economic benefits will be received

Contract costs to complete can be measured reliably

Stage of completion can be measured reliably

Contract costs to date can be identified and measured reliably

Treatment

In year 1, identify the costs incurred, calculate the profit and insert revenue as the balancing figure

In the following years, do the same on a cumulative basis and then deduct amounts recognised in previous years

Cost-plus contract – estimate of outcome is reliable if

Probable that the economic benefits associated with the contract will be received by the entity

Total costs can be clearly identified and reliably measured

Treatment

In year 1, identify the costs to be recognised in cost of sales, calculate the profit and insert revenue as a balancing figure

In the following years, do the same on a cumulative basis and then deduct amounts recognised in previous years

Estimate of outcome is not reliable

Contract costs should be recognised immediately and revenue should only be recognised to the extent that it is probable that the costs are recoverable from the customer

No profit is recognised prior to the outcome of the contract being reliably estimated

A loss is recognised immediately if costs incurred cannot be recovered from the customer

Expected losses

Recognise the loss immediately in the P&L

Such a loss should be recognised even if work on the contract has not yet been commenced

Revenue should be recognised based on the stage of completion – cost of sales will therefore be a balancing figure between revenue and the loss which needs to be recognised immediately

The difference between costs incurred and cost of sales should be recognised as a provision for losses and become part of the gross amounts due from/to customers

Judgements required

Combining of contracts – if one is profitable and the other is loss-making then combining them into a single contract will result in a loss being offset against the profit – management should not hide loss-making contracts

Estimation of the stage of completion of each contract

Costs to be incurred in the future

Additional revenue to be recovered from the customer as a result of variations in the contract

Disclosures

If you have the figures available and your estimated mark allocation suggests that there are marks available then you may wish to consider including the following breakdown:

Gross amounts due from customers and due to customers

Costs incurred to date	X
Add profit recognised	X
Less losses recognised on contract	(X)
Less progress billings made	(X)
	X/(X)

If the total is positive, this amount due from customers is recognised as a current asset in the SFP

If the total is negative, this amount is due to customers (excess billings) and is recognised as a current liability in the SFP

Construction contract pro formas

Cost-plus

In year 1, identify costs, calculate the profit based on the mark up and then insert revenue as a balancing figure

Repeat the process for the following years on a cumulative basis (i.e. using all the costs incurred to that date) but remember to allow for amounts recognised in previous years for costs, revenue and profit

Fixed price (assuming that a profitable outcome of the contract can be estimated reliably)

	Year 1	Year 2	Year 3
Contract costs incurred to date	110	320	450
Estimated costs to complete	250	120	0
Total contract costs	360	440	450
Profit	120	100	130

Answering technique

Identify the costs incurred based on stage of completion, calculate the profit based on stage of completion and insert revenue as the balancing figure.

Year 1 – the project is 110 / 360 or 31% complete (year 1 costs / total contract costs expected)

Therefore recognise 31% of expected project profit (31% x 120 = 37.2) and add this to the costs incurred of 110 to derive the revenue figure of 147.2.

Year 2 – the project is 320 / 440 or 73% complete

Therefore recognise 73% of expected project profit (73% x 100 = 73) and apply this to the cumulative costs incurred of 320 to derive a cumulative revenue figure of 393.

However, we have **already recognised** some amounts in the prior year so we need to adjust the costs, profit and revenue figures to reflect the change in this year's figures only

Costs to recognise this year (320 – 110 PY)	210
Profit to recognise this year only (73 – 37.2 PY)	35.8
Revenue to recognise this year (balancing figure or 393 – 147.2 PY)	245.8

(The above figures are subject to rounding – this would not affect your mark in the examination.)

Customer loyalty programmes

Suggested mark allocation in an FR question (CR Q2): 4 marks

Treatment

IFRIC 13 requires that reward points are treated as a separate element of a sale

Measure the reward points at the FV to the customer, based on the amount for which they could be sold separately

This amount should be deferred and recognised in revenue when the reward points are redeemed

Customers are treated as implicitly paying for the reward points when they buy other goods and services – therefore some of the revenue should be allocated to the points

Not all customers will redeem their points so apply a proportion to the total FV e.g. if only one in three customers is expected to redeem their points then multiply the total FV by 1/3

Add the amounts from the above step to the consideration received – this means the company will effectively have sold goods worth more than the consideration but have only received the consideration itself

Therefore **gross down** the consideration by a fraction based on the addition of the reward points

Example – a company receives consideration of £50m but provides reward points with a FV of £5m and it is expected that two in five customers will redeem their points

2 / 5 x £5m = £2m adjusted FV of the reward points

Company has made sales of £50m + £2m or £52m but has only received £50m

Allocate 50 / 52 x 50 or **£48.07m** to revenue for the year and the balance of **£1.93m** is deferred until the reward points are redeemed

Deferred tax

Suggested mark allocation in an FR question (CR Q2): 2 marks per issue (therefore work quickly and aim to at least cover all issues to some extent rather than concentrating on only certain areas)

Treatment

Choice of tax rate to apply

IAS 12 states that the tax rate to be used is the rate expected to apply when the asset is realised or the liability settled

This should be based upon laws already **enacted** or **substantively enacted** by the year end

Journals

To record an increase in a deferred tax asset

Debit   Deferred tax asset (SFP) – consider whether a current or non-current asset

Credit Tax charge (P&L*)

To record an increase in a deferred tax liability

Debit   Tax charge (P&L*)

Credit Deferred tax liability (SFP) – consider whether a current or non-current liability

* Note that if the underlying transaction is recognised in equity through OCI, then the resulting deferred tax is included in OCI rather than the P&L as the deferred tax follows the underlying accounting treatment – for example, AFS investments

Development costs

Check the question wording carefully to determine how these are treated in the foreign country

In many cases, the expenses are allowed for tax purposes at the time they are paid – however, for accounts purposes, if the costs are being capitalised then they will not be deducted for accounting profit purposes until the project commences and amortisation is charged

The **tax benefit** has therefore been taken **before** the **accounting benefit** and so a deferred tax **liability** arises, based on the carrying amount of the project valued at the applicable tax rate

Fair value adjustments on a business combination

IFRS 3 requires recognition of net assets at FV but a revaluation upwards does not change the tax base of an asset – the revaluation is only recognised by tax authorities on disposal or generation of taxable income from the asset

A **revaluation upwards** therefore results in a **deferred tax liability** in the group financial statements – this will **increase** goodwill because there will be a bigger difference between consideration paid and the net assets acquired (since we have now found another liability to deduct from the net assets)

The liability will be equal to the difference between the revalued carrying amount and the unchanged tax base, multiplied by the relevant tax rate

Note that if the revaluation is recognised in OCI (e.g. revaluation of PPE) then the related deferred tax adjustment should also be recognised through OCI

Example – an asset with a carrying amount of 6 is revalued to its FV of 8 as part of a business combination

The carrying amount in the group financial statements will be 8 but the tax base will remain at 6 so there is a temporary difference of 2, to be valued at the tax rate applicable to the entity

No adjustment is required in the company's **individual** accounts as no FV adjustment is required – this matter only affects the **group accounts**

Recognition of goodwill on acquisition does not give rise to any deferred tax

Leases

In the case of a finance lease, the asset is written off over its useful life and a finance cost is recognised at a constant rate on the carrying amount of the liability

For tax purposes, relief is normally given as rentals are paid – the **tax base is nil** as there is no asset (TWDV value) for tax purposes and relief will be given in future as payments are made

Therefore there is likely to be a **deferred tax asset**, representing the tax recoverable in future – total rental payments which are deductible for tax purposes are likely to exceed the total depreciation of the asset because the rental payments must cover the costs of purchasing the asset and also cover the finance charge on top of the cost of the asset itself whereas depreciation is based only on the initial capitalised amount and does not include any element of finance charge

Tax losses – future expected profitability

It may be possible to recognise a **deferred tax asset** of an amount equal to tax losses incurred, valued at the applicable tax rate

However, there must be a **reasonable prospect of future profitability** – the deferred tax asset can only be recognised **to the extent that the losses are likely to be offset against future profits** (but subject to the January 2017 amendment discussed in the next sub-section)

Therefore, if it appears that the entity is unlikely to realise profits in the future due to poor underlying performance, no deferred tax asset should be recognised

It may be necessary to recognise only **some** of the losses as a deferred tax asset i.e. only to the extent that they can be matched with likely future profits – this is quite a common point in the exam and could link into auditing/ethics if there is a suggestion that management are being too optimistic about future profitability in order to boost the company's asset base and/or in order to take a Credit to the P&L in relation to the deferred tax asset as a way of boosting accounting profit

Tax losses – company reporting a tax loss (January 2017 amendment)

Under an amendment effective from January 2017, a special calculation is performed to determine the deferred tax asset for a company reporting a tax loss – see the following example, which is based on the example on page 1195 and page 1196 of the 2018 Corporate Reporting Study Manual

A company has a deductible temporary difference of £400,000 and a taxable temporary difference of £120,000. The company expects the bottom line of its tax return to show a tax loss of £80,000.

Step 1 – determine whether there is a **taxable temporary difference** to support the recognition of a deferred tax asset – the company has a taxable temporary difference of **£120,000** so **at least** this amount can be recognised as a deferred tax asset

Step 2 – special calculation of taxable profit for recognition test

Expected tax loss per bottom line of tax return	(80)
less reversing taxable temporary difference	(120)
plus reversing deductible temporary difference	400
Taxable profit for recognition test	200

Step 3 – add together amounts from **Steps 1** and **2** – the company can therefore recognise a deferred tax asset of £120,000 + £200,000 = £320,000

This should be valued at the relevant tax rate.

This deferred tax asset would be recognised even though the company has an expected loss in its tax return.

Pensions – P&L and OCI split

In many tax jurisdictions, **pensions** are only **deductible** for **tax purposes** when **actually paid out** to recipients

A deferred tax **asset** will arise on the difference between the **net pension liability** and the **tax base of nil** (no tax deduction until actually paid in a future period)

In practice, most pension schemes record a net pension **liability** (i.e. a large amount to pay out in future, which will yield future tax deductibility) so there will be a deferred tax **asset** adjustment at the year end – the Credit side of this adjustment will go to the P&L

Remember that **actuarial gains and losses** must be recognised through **OCI** and deferred tax adjustments **follow** the accounting treatment so **deferred tax adjustments** on **actuarial gains and losses** must **also** be recognised through **OCI**

In practice, most pension schemes record an actuarial **loss** for the year, so there will be a deferred tax **asset** adjustment which goes through **OCI**

You may therefore have to carefully split an overall deferred tax asset adjustment into its P&L and OCI **components** (credit the P&L in relation to the net pension liability element **and** OCI in relation to the actuarial loss element)– see Corporate Reporting Question Bank Q2 **Mervyn** for an example of this process

PPE

The **accounting carrying amount** of PPE is the **net book value** of the assets – this is reduced gradually based on **depreciation**

The **tax base** is the tax written down value – this is reduced gradually based on the **capital allowance** rate

It is unlikely that the depreciation rate will be the same as the capital allowance rate – this gives rise to a temporary difference

If the **tax base exceeds the carrying amount**, there will be a **deferred tax asset** as over the remaining life of the asset there will be more tax deductions received (which would reduce taxable profits) than depreciation to add back (which would increase taxable profits) – overall, the entity will see a **net deduction** from the tax charge

If the **tax base is lower than the carrying amount**, there will be a **deferred tax liability** as over the remaining life of the asset there will be fewer tax deductions (which would reduce taxable profits) than depreciation to add back (which would increase taxable profits) – overall, the entity will see a **net addition** to the tax charge. Put another way, too much tax relief has already been granted relative to the accounts carrying amount and this needs to be reversed

Calculate the difference between the carrying amount and tax base at the year end and create a deferred tax asset or liability as required, per the above. Then check to see what the opening liability or asset was – only the necessary **change** is charged this year.

PPE – Revaluation

This creates a **deferred tax liability** – there is no increase in the tax base from a revaluation but the carrying amount in the accounts will increase

The charge to increase the deferred tax liability should be recognised in **OCI** and not in **profit or loss**

Interaction with IAS 40

If the property is held under the FV model, gains are recognised through **profit or loss** and taxable at the same time (or in the case of a loss, allowable for tax at the same time) so there is **no deferred tax** to consider as there is **no timing mismatch** – however, if the item is held under the cost model or the revaluation model under IAS 16 then revaluation gains are recognised through OCI and therefore are not taxed at the time, giving rise to a deferred tax liability – remember that this deferred tax should follow the underlying item and be recognised in OCI and not in the current tax account in the P&L

Provisions

Often provisions will relate to future accounting periods (remember to apply discounting if this would make a material difference) – an expense will be **recognised** for accounting purposes but the amounts will not be deductible for **tax purposes** until they are actually paid in **future**

The entity will therefore receive a **future tax benefit** so a **deferred tax asset** is created, based on the estimated present value of the provision value at the applicable tax rate

Share-based payment

Normally, **tax** authorities do not give relief for share-based payments **until exercise** – this contrasts with the accounts treatment where there will be an **annual expense** posted with an equivalent increase in equity to be issued (or liabilities for a cash-settled scheme) each year

This will create a **deferred tax asset** because the entity will have a future tax deduction which has not yet been claimed

The accounts carrying amount of the share-based payment expense will be nil because the expense is recognised in full each year

The tax base of the share-based payments will be based on

> options x employees x proportion of employees expected to qualify x intrinsic value x fraction for the relevant year (e.g. 1/3 in the first year of a 3 year vesting period, 2/3 in the second year and so on)

> Intrinsic value is the difference between the market price and the exercise price under the option

Therefore the temporary difference will be **equal to the tax base** as the carrying amount for accounts purposes is **nil**

Deferred tax that relates to the **excess** of intrinsic value over fair value at the grant date should be recognised in **equity** – therefore if the tax deduction **exceeds** the accounting deduction put the excess through **equity** and not the P&L

Unrealised profit (PURPs)

The tax authorities tax a sale regardless of whether it is internal or external to the group – taxation is based on individual company profit figures, not the group figures

In the group accounts, unrealised profits on goods sold internally which remain in inventories must be cancelled – this means that the accounts carrying amount of inventory in the group accounts will be lower than the tax base of those inventories, because of the deduction of the PURP

Therefore there will be a **deferred tax asset** equal to the difference between the carrying amount in the group accounts and the tax base, valued at the tax rate applicable to the entity – the reason is that the tax authorities will **already have charged tax** on sales of those inventories because the fact that the sales were intra-group is not relevant for tax purposes: the group can therefore earn future profits without incurring tax so a **deferred tax asset arises** – therefore it is necessary to reduce the group's tax charge to match the accounting treatment where profit was reduced when adjusting for the PURP

This is because tax has been charged on profit which is non-existent from the group perspective

Unremitted earnings

Unremitted earnings potentially create a deferred tax liability – the group accounts consolidate the profit of subsidiaries but this is not recognised for tax purposes: rather, additional tax could be due when the earnings are remitted from the subsidiary to the parent

However, IAS 12 states that no deferred tax liability should be recognised if the parent company controls the timing of the subsidiary's dividend distribution and it is probable that the temporary difference will not reverse in the foreseeable future as the parent intends to leave the profits within the subsidiary for reinvestment purposes

DEPS

Suggested mark allocation in an FR question (CR Q2): 4-5 marks

Provides useful information to users by relating **current** earnings to the possible **future** capital structure (i.e. future number of shares that could exist)

DEPS allows for both the impact on earnings of the issued shares and also the impact of an increased number of shares

Could be used as part of a PE valuation to show the impact on future valuation if instruments are converted into equity

Limitations

Uses **current** earnings but **future** number of shares – the current earnings figure may not be relevant in future years – the level of earnings at the time of conversion is what matters

Assumes that all potential diluting financial instruments will be converted into shares – this may not happen as some debt holders may redeem the instrument for cash, rather than converting into shares, or share options may lapse if holders leave the company

DEPS can therefore only be an **indicator** regarding potential future events – it is not a **forecast** of future earnings

Antidilution

If potential ordinary shares would **increase** EPS (or decrease the loss per share) then they are **antidilutive** and are not taken into account for DEPS purposes

Each issue or series of potential ordinary shares is considered **separately** rather than in aggregate

Ignore any shares that increase EPS or decrease the loss per share as these are automatically antidilutive

Rank dilutive instruments from most to least dilutive – options and warrants are generally included first because they do not affect the numerator (top half) of the calculation – dilutive factors are added one by one into the DEPS calculation in order to identify the maximum dilution

Calculation of diluted earnings

Take profit or loss attributable to **ordinary** equity holders and adjust this for the **after-tax** effect of

Any dividends or other items relating to dilutive potential ordinary shares deducted in arriving at profit or loss attributable to ordinary equity holders

Any interest recognised in the period relating to dilutive potential ordinary shares

Any other changes in income or expense that would result from the conversion of the dilutive potential ordinary shares

Calculation of number of shares

Treat dilution as occurring at the **start of the period** or, if later, the date of issue of the potential ordinary shares

If there is more than one basis of conversion then assume the most advantageous rate of conversion from the standpoint of the holder

Convertible instruments

Increase earnings by interest saved, net of tax

Increase number of shares by the number of shares created by the conversion

Options and warrants (other than employee share options)

Apply a split calculation – shares issued at average market price are ignored but **free shares** are added into the calculation

Calculation of "free shares" – example

Exercise price is £0.50, average market price is £1.50 and number of shares under option is 600,000

Free element is £1.00 / £1.50 x 600,000 or 400,000

Ignore the other 200,000 shares for DEPS purposes

Employee share options

In the case of vested shares, apply a "free share" approach as above (see Options and warrants above)

In the case of unvested shares, apply the same general method but first find the per share amount still to be recognised in the P&L relating to the share options and add this to the exercise price in the calculation before proceeding as normal using a free shares calculation

Example

Exercise price is £21 in relation to 5m shares with £15m to be recognised – average market price is £30

The per share amount still to be recognised is £15m / 5m = £3 so exercise price now treated as £21 + £3 or £24

"Free shares" therefore based on £30 - £24 = 6 / 30 x shares under option

Contingently issuable shares

Do not include in EPS unless actually issued

Include for DEPS if and only if the conditions leading to their issue are satisfied, treating the end of the current accounting period as if it were the end of the contingency period (i.e. look at whether the conditions would be satisfied assuming that nothing were to change between the current accounting period and ultimate end date)

If necessary to include, include from the beginning of the period, or, if later, from the date of the contingent share agreement if this was entered into during the year

Examples of performance criteria: future earnings, market price of shares, future earnings & market price of shares

If the performance criteria involve a **cumulative target** then no dilution is accounted for until the cumulative target has been met – for example, for a target of **average profits of £100,000 over 5 years** then the cumulative target required is £500,000 so no DEPS impact occurs until the cumulative target is met i.e. towards the end of the process rather than each year

As always with DEPS, assume that the shares were issued at the **start** of the year (only assume a later date if the agreement was entered into during the current accounting period)

Equity-settled share scheme

Normally it is necessary to take account of the number of "free" shares being allocated, assuming that the whole scheme will vest

Where options are not yet vested, there should also be an adjustment to the option exercise price based on the remaining IFRS 2 cost to be expensed in future – calculate what this is on a per share basis and add it to the exercise price before calculating the number of "free shares" in the normal way (see previous page)

If there is a **performance condition** (other than the mere passage of time) such as a share price condition then treat the shares as contingently issuable shares

> IAS 33 states that "the calculation of diluted EPS is based on the number of ordinary shares that would be issued if the market price at the end of the reporting period were the market price at the end of the contingency period" – therefore it is possible that there may not be dilution if the condition is not met at the year end

See also our section on **EPS** starting on page 51.

Derivatives and Embedded Derivatives

Suggested mark allocation in an FR question (CR Q2): 4 marks

Derivative – Definition

Value changes in response to the change in price of an underlying security, commodity, currency, index or other financial instrument(s)

Initial net investment is zero or is small in relation to the value of the underlying security or index

Settled on a future date

Tips

Make sure you always review the above 3 criteria for a derivative to exist – make sure you connect these to the scenario through **examples**

Accounting treatment

Recognise a derivative initially at fair value – do not forget to add on the **initial cost**, if any (see below), but do not add any **transaction fees**

Dr Financial asset

Cr Cash/Payables

Treat any **transaction** costs as an expense in the P&L – however, the **cost of the instrument** itself (e.g. a **premium** on an option) should be **capitalised** into the cost of the asset on the SFP i.e. it should **not** be expensed – therefore just expense **transaction costs** such as professional fees

Update the instrument for fair value at the SFP date – the change in fair value should be recognised in profit or loss

Example of the journals for a **gain** on a derivative in the year

Dr Financial asset

Cr Operating income (P&L)

Example of the journals for a **loss** on a derivative in the year

Dr Operating income (P&L)

Cr Financial asset

Physical delivery versus net settlement

If the contract has been used partially or entirely for **business purposes** and thus **physical delivery** is taken, then the instrument would be **scoped out** of IAS 39 and **not** treated as a **derivative**

This could happen if there is an established past practice of taking physical delivery for use in the business

However, if there is **any** intention for "net settlement" then this would imply that the instrument is not being used for business usage and therefore it **should** be treated as a **derivative** under IAS 39

Embedded Derivatives – Definition

A derivative component of a hybrid (combined) instrument that also includes a non-derivative host contract

Exam tip – if the exam paper provides you with a **separately** stated FV of an instrument if it were purchased on its own then this is a strong indicator that an **embedded** derivative exists as you are being given a figure to **split out**

Example host contracts

Leases, debt or equity instruments, insurance contracts, sale or purchase contracts, construction contracts

The contract must involve terms such that the embedded derivative cannot be detached and sold to a third party – if it can be, it is simply a separate financial instrument

Treatment

Determine (1) if the **economic** characteristics and risks of the embedded derivative are **not closely related** to the economic characteristics and risks of the host contract (2) a **separate** instrument with the **same terms** as the embedded derivative would meet the definition of a derivative and (3) the **hybrid contract** is not already being accounted for at FVtPL

Separate out the derivative from its host contract and treat as a normal derivative – this ensures that the entity cannot **hide** the derivative outside of the P&L

The entity may **choose** to **designate** a hybrid contract at FVtPL, avoiding the need to **split out** the embedded derivative

Examples of embedded derivatives/not closely related instruments

Cash flows of the host contract are modified by an index, specified interest rate, foreign exchange rate, index of price or rates etc – i.e. something which has no real connection with the contract

Convertible bond – a mixture of a normal bond (host contract) and a call option (embedded derivative) that gives the holder of the bond the right to exchange the bond for shares in the company

Currency involved is different from the functional currency of both parties (unless the items in the transaction are routinely denominated in the currency involved in international commerce)

Option to extend the term on a fixed debt instrument without resetting the interest rate to market rates

Credit derivatives in a debt instrument

Put option enabling the holder to require the issuer to reacquire the instrument for a value that varies on the basis of a change in an equity or commodity price or index

From the point of view of the holder only, a call option embedded in an equity instrument that enables the issuer to reacquire that equity instrument at a specified price

Equity-indexed interest or principal payments embedded in a host debt instrument or insurance contract

An equity conversion feature embedded in a convertible debt instrument

A call, put or prepayment option embedded in a host debt contract or host insurance contract

Distributable Profits

The basic rule

Distributable profits are accumulated realised profits less accumulated realised losses

For **listed** companies, distributable profits are **further** reduced by the excess of unrealised losses over unrealised profits

Listed companies must also not make a distribution if this reduces net assets below the total of called-up share capital and undistributable reserves

Undistributable reserves are the share premium account, net unrealised profits and other reserve specified by law or the company's constitution to be unrealised e.g. a capital redemption reserve

Realised or unrealised?

Companies Act 2006 provides specific guidance.

A provision is a realised loss

A revaluation surplus is an unrealised profit

Additional depreciation on revalued non-current assets can be added back to profits for the purposes of determining distributable amounts

Where a revalued asset is disposed of, the unrealised surplus or loss on revaluation becomes a realised profit or loss

Revaluation gains are unrealised unless they reverse a loss previously treated as realised

Losses are realised except where the loss offsets a previous surplus on the same asset or arises on a revaluation of all non-current assets or arises on a revaluation of some non-current assets where the directors consider that the assets not revalued are worth at least their book value

ICAEW/ICAS Technical Release 02/10

The translation of monetary assets which comprise qualifying consideration or a liability denominated in a foreign currency is a realised profit

Goodwill arising in a company's individual financial statements will become a realised loss as the goodwill is amortised or written down for impairment in accordance with the relevant accounting standards

Negative goodwill (gain on a bargain purchase) up to the FV of the non-monetary assets acquired should be treated as being realised in the periods in which the non-monetary assets are recovered, whether through depreciation or sale

Group calculation?

The calculation must be done for each entity separately and not for the consolidated group – the consolidated group only exists for accounting purposes

Note that the legality of a dividend distribution is determined by the distributable profits in the **separate** financial statements of a single company rather than by **consolidated** retained earnings

It is possible for group retained earnings to be negative due to losses in subsidiaries but with an individual parent company having a positive retained earnings balance due to its own profitability – this would allow payment of a dividend to the parent company's shareholders

EPS

Suggested mark allocation in an FR question (CR Q2): 2 marks

Compliance with IAS 33 on EPS is mandatory for the **separate** financial statements of entities whose ordinary shares are **publicly traded** or are in the **process of being issued** in public markets and for the **consolidated** financial statements for groups whose parent has shares similarly traded/being issued

Other entities need not present EPS – if their shares are not traded there is no readily available market price to calculate the PE ratio (the reason why EPS figures are quoted)

Presentation

EPS should be presented in the P&L (DEPS should also be presented with equal prominence, if needed)

Basic calculation

Profit or loss attributable to ordinary equity holders of the parent / weighted average number of ordinary shares outstanding during the period

To calculate the profit or loss figure used here, remember to treat **redeemable** preference shares as liabilities and as such these involve a **finance charge** that should **already have been deducted** in the P&L (so no adjustment needed if the client has used the right approach) – but remember to then deduct the amount of any **dividend on irredeemable** preference shares (as EPS works on the basis of profit or loss attributable to **ordinary** shares)

In the case of cumulative dividends on irredeemable preference shares then

> If the dividend is not paid in the year, deduct it from profit for the EPS calculation

> When the arrears of past dividends are paid, exclude from the EPS calculation

Rights issue

See separate **Rights issue** topic on page 159.

Bonus fraction

The terms work on the basis for "new for old" – a 2 for 1 bonus issue means that 2 new shares are issued for every 1 existing or old share already held – the bonus fraction would then be 3 / 1 (holder now has 3 shares and had 1 before)

Remember that this should always have a **higher** number on the top of the fraction than on the **bottom** of the fraction

Remember to treat bonus issues as if the relevant shares have always existed i.e. go right back in time over the full current year and also as against the prior year

Remember that a quick way to find the **prior year** comparative EPS after a bonus issue is to apply the **reciprocal** of the fraction to last year's **EPS** – this will have the effect of pushing down last year's EPS as we are now assuming that more shares always existed (with earnings last year unchanged, EPS must now be lower when allowing for the new bonus shares as the same amount of earnings is being spread over a greater number of shares)

Careful – if you are told last year's **earnings** (rather than **EPS**) then you cannot use this reciprocal approach – instead you will need to calculate the total number of shares and divide last year's earnings by that number of shares – therefore always check carefully whether you have been told EPS or rather total earnings

Issue at full market price

Only consider this on a **prospective** basis – do **not** go backwards and update the number of shares

There is no need for any complicated fraction as with a bonus or rights issue – simply add in the number of shares from the relevant date and pro-rate this (as the issue will almost certainly happen during the year)

Profit attributable to ordinary equity holders

Profit after tax after the deduction of preference dividends and other financing costs

Partly paid shares

Treat these as a fraction of a share, based on their ability to participate in dividends

So if 600 shares are issued at a £4 price but only £2 has been paid than apply a fraction of 2 / 4 to the share issue, treating it as an issue of 300 shares (not 600)

See also our section on **DEPS** starting on page 43

Ethics

Suggested mark allocation in an FR question (CR Q2): 5-6 marks

The 5 threats

Intimidation threat

Self-interest threat

Self-review threat

Management threat

Advocacy threat

The 5 ICAEW Code Principles

Integrity – being straightforward and honest in all professional and business relationships

Objectivity – not allowing bias, conflicts of interest or undue influence of others to override a professional judgement

Professional competence and due care – only perform work that one is competent to perform

Confidentiality – not to disclose information to third parties without proper and specific authority

Professional behaviour – compliance with laws and regulations and avoidance of any action that discredits the profession

Fee income levels

Revised Ethical Standard 2016 upper bound of 15% of the firm's total fee income from an unlisted client

For a listed or Public Interest Entity (PIE) client, the limit falls to 10%

If fees range from 5% to 10% for listed/PIE clients or 10% to 15% for non-listed clients, the fact needs to be disclosed to the ethics partner and those charged with governance at the client – appropriate safeguards should be adopted, including declining some of the work

Application of pressure to the auditor – materiality, fees, timing

Auditors must act in the public interest as they have responsibilities to the users of the financial statements

Objectivity is threatened if there is pressure to increase materiality and reduce the amount of work required – professional judgement is threatened – auditor must determine materiality in an objective way, considering the needs of the users of the financial statements

Self-interest threat as auditor will want to retain work in future years but the client is requesting a reduction in audit time and costs to retain margin – must ensure that the auditor is not influenced by the wish to retain future work

Intimidation threat as client is suggesting that auditor may not be given other non-audit work in future – this could prevent objectivity and safeguards will need to be applied – risk of "low-balling" on audit work in order to win non-audit work

Actions: discuss with ethics partner at an early stage and arrange for an additional partner file review – advice from ICAEW ethics helpline – full documentation of any decisions on level of work and contentious issues – consider making changes to ensure an appropriate level and resilience of the audit team

Late appointment as auditor

Check if this has occurred because of the resignation of a previous auditor – if this is the case, perhaps an issue was identified by that auditor and we should determine if this matter still applies – this should be discussed with the client

Ensure that adequate professional clearance has been obtained from the previous auditor and that there are no matters of which we should be aware

Ensure that satisfactory client identification procedures have been performed

Check if we have been appointed as auditor after the year end – if this is the case, it may be more difficult to assess matters as they stood at the year-end – if we cannot implement audit procedures to gain sufficient audit evidence of the position at the year-end then the audit opinion will have to be modified

> If the possible errors are considered to be material, this may result in a qualified or "except for" opinion

> If the potential effect is pervasive, we may have to issue a "disclaimer" of opinion

Acting as auditor during a possible takeover or within a group – confidentiality

As auditors of an entity, we may have access to confidential information which would be of use to another party in assessing the value or probability of various matters e.g. the probability of contingent consideration being payable or the fair value of assets and liabilities

This creates a conflict of interest – we must ensure that confidential information cannot be passed from one company to the other

Within a group situation, the potential conflict of interest should be disclosed to the relevant audit committee

It may be necessary to arrange independent partner reviews of the group and individual entity audit files

Personal relationships between audit team members and client staff

If an individual is considered to be a close family member, then the member of the audit team may have to be removed from the team, particularly if the family member has a role such as a financial controller or director at the client – this is because the family member could exercise influence over the information submitted for audit

It would not matter if the close family member used to work for the audit firm unless he or she was a partner of the firm, in which case the audit appointment should not be accepted

Quality of work performed

The adviser must act in accordance with the ethical code in respect of professional competence and due care

Inadequate supervision of a junior member of staff would compromise the quality of work, especially if not identified on a timely basis – if there are problems on other assignments involving the same individual, this would be a further concern

Any evidence of poor or inadequate training would also suggest a lack of professional competence

Possible fraud

The auditor needs to determine whether there is collusion between staff and/or other entities (if applicable)

There is an ethical issue for the auditor if the client has unaddressed ethical issues as this increases engagement risk

The auditor should adopt an attitude of professional scepticism – the auditor should obtain relevant audit evidence of the impact of fraud-related issues and this should be documented including tests performed, discussions with audit team members and detailed enquiries made at the appropriate level of management together with their responses

If fraud is suspected, the entity should report to those responsible for governance at the appropriate level – note that key finance staff such as finance directors or finance controllers could be involved in the fraud so their actions should be given careful consideration

There may also be responsibilities under the money laundering legislation so there should be consultation with the firm's MLRO

Requesting the audit firm to assist in calculating entries

This would require the audit firm to ensure any threat of self-review can be mitigated

This can be achieved by using people from outside the audit team to assist or suggesting that parent company staff rather than audit firm staff provide assistance

The audit firm should also ensure that the financial controller and directors take full managerial responsibility for all assumptions made – in particular this includes judgemental assumptions which must definitely not be suggested by the audit firm or the firm will be playing a management role

Further ethical problems will arise if client staff lack expertise in a complex area – the auditor should be even more alert to the risks of misstatement and the fact that the audit firm may be asked to step in as this would lead to a management threat

Audit firm to provide additional assurance services

Such an assignment would be called a "non-audit related service"

The firm should identify any threats to independence and objectivity

A low fee for the work could be a threat to independence

The relative size of the engagement fee in relation to the audit fee should be considered and discussed with the ethics partner

There may also be a risk that the firm would end up auditing its own work

Consider if the firm is being pressurised by the client in any way

The firm should not undertake work in which it does not have the expertise – ICAEW Chartered Accountants must act in accordance with professional competence and behaviour

The firm must consider the nature of the non-audit services involved – further information may be required on timing, nature and extent of the work, likely level of fees and the fee basis

Must guard against "low-balling" on audit work in order to win non-audit work

Acting on overheard information

Overheard information contains no actual evidence and could be no more than malicious gossip without foundation in fact

Even so, the accountant who has heard the information is not entitled to ignore it completely – the accountant should investigate the allegations as discreetly as possible – there may be a criminal dimension

If the issue could be defined as money laundering then the accountant must take care that enquiries do not "tip off" any relevant individuals

Once the relevant facts have been gathered, it may be appropriate to escalate the matter – it may be worth contacting ICAEW for help in determining whether or not the matter should be taken forward, what kind of evidence is required and what action would be most appropriate

All ICAEW Chartered Accountants are bound by the ICAEW Ethical Code and must act with integrity in all circumstances and must display professional behaviour – otherwise this could bring the profession into disrepute

There may be internal procedures to deal with the allegations at the client company – if the company is listed it should have appointed Non-Executive Directors but if it is unlisted it may still have such Directors

It may be appropriate to approach the chair of the audit committee, provided that the accountant is very certain of the facts and the allegations are presented carefully

At all stages a detailed record of investigations, deliberations and conclusions may be required as evidence in the event of criminal and/or professional disciplinary action

Identification of errors in corporation tax return

Must follow the fundamental principles of the ICAEW code – must not be associated with a tax return which the accountant knows to contain an error

Should report this to HMRC

Where a matter is in the public interest, duty to report to ICAEW any facts or matters indicating that a member or trainee member may have become liable to disciplinary action – deliberate underpayment of tax cannot be in the public interest so there may well be a duty to report

Disciplinary action could take place if the accountant does not act within the spirit of the Code

Ask the client to disclose the error to the tax authority – if there is a refusal, the matter should be raised with those charged with governance at the client

Consider whether to continue to act for a client which has knowingly filed a false tax return

Consult the ethics partner throughout the deliberations

Could be reporting implications under the Money Laundering regulations because tax evasion results in criminal property – MLRO should be consulted on whether disclosure to the NCA is needed – ensure no tipping off

Ensure that an appropriately experienced and skilled individual performs the audit work on tax balances as these are not straightforward

If the client refuses to make adjustment, this potentially raises an intimidation threat – discuss with the assignment partner and the firm's ethics partner – raise the matter with those charged with governance and the relevant adjustments should be made to the financial statements

Other key threats: self-interest (fees from client), self-review (auditing tax computations it had prepared), management (auditor might become involved in tax planning – tax is a very technical area so can management be properly informed?)

Consider whether the audit firm wants to be associated with such a client, taking into account other errors – consider resignation

Dominance of a Board member

Creates a governance issue but not necessarily an ethical issue

Needs to be separation between Chairperson and CEO

No Finance Director in place

Need to ensure a Finance Director is in place rather than having CEO making all decisions

This could lead to ethical concerns such as pressure to produce good results or there may be a lack of good quality information and controls – there may also be an opportunity for people to make the most of the fact that an individual with significant supervisory responsibilities over controls is not in place

Greater likelihood of a management threat for the audit firm if it acts in the role of a Finance Director

Taxation issues – transfer pricing

Special deals with unusual rental fees may have been entered into to evade UK tax

Details and expert input from tax consultants in the overseas country needed

Report to the audit firm's Money Laundering Reporting Officer may be required

AIM-listed company

Not required to make disclosures of compliance with the provisions of the UK Corporate Governance Code

ISA 260 requires matters of concern to be raised with those charged with governance – audit committee would be the point of contact

Information in the published financial statements should be reviewed for consistency with appropriate professional scepticism being applied

Cyber attack with less than full transparency from the client

Background: possible security breach so client accounts may have been accessed, but no evidence so far and therefore clients not informed – some clients might suffer a financial loss – disclosed in management commentary in the interim financial statements but not made public in any other way

Answer: appears to be a deliberate attempt to hold back information from the company's clients – could be a breach of requirements regarding the protection of client data

Lack of transparency, professional competence and due care – attempt by FD (ICAEW Chartered Accountant) to cover up could indicate weak corporate governance

Taken with other matters (management commentary states that gross profit margin has increased from 60% but does not say what figure it has increased to, prepayment of costs and bringing forward income), could suggest that FD is attempting to manipulate the accounts

Self-interest threat for assurance provider as will not want to jeopardise relationship with client

Actions: engagement partner should discuss with client's directors to establish the facts – consult ethics partner to consider whether there is a case for reporting a fellow ICAEW member (the FD at the client) for a breach of the ICAEW Code – assurance provider should seek legal advice and could suffer reputational damage

Events After the Reporting Period

Suggested mark allocation in an FR question (CR Q2): 5 marks

Treatment

The event provides evidence of **conditions** that **existed** at the **end of the reporting period** – IAS 10 therefore applies

An accrual may be needed if we now have good evidence of the costs involved

Note that this could mean that a contingent liability in the draft accounts is now replaced and its related note removed as we have better evidence of the position as it stood at the end of the reporting period

There is no specific requirement to disclose the mere fact that the event is an adjusting event

Adjusting events after the reporting period (evidence of conditions at the reporting date)

Settlement of a court case that confirms that the entity had an obligation at the reporting date

Evidence that an asset was impaired at the reporting date e.g. bankruptcy of a customer or selling prices for inventory now sold

Determination of bonus payments or a profit-sharing agreement for the year

Finalisation of prices for assets sold/purchased before the year end

Discovery of material fraud or errors that show the financial statements are misstated

Adjustment to EPS for bonus issues, share splits or share consolidations where the number of shares changed without an increase in resources – the additional shares issued are treated as having been in issue for the whole period

Non-adjusting events after the reporting period (evidence of conditions that arose after the reporting date)

Such events should be disclosed where this would influence the economic decisions made by users of the financial statements but there is no need to recognise the amounts

A major business combination after the reporting date

Announcement of plan to discontinue an operation

Major purchases and disposals of assets

Classification of assets as held for sale

Expropriation of assets by government

Destruction of assets

Announcing or commencing the implementation of a major restructuring

Major ordinary share transactions (unless no inflow or outflow of economic resources is involved)

Decline in the market value of investments including investment properties after the reporting date – these should not be affected by hindsight

Examples from past papers

Court case

If the court case was in progress at the year-end but has now been concluded and a specific monetary amount is known then an adjusting event occurs – we have good evidence of the cost of a matter in progress at the year end

Proposed dividend

Dividends are only recognised if they are declared before the end of the reporting period

The directors do not have any obligation to declare or pay a dividend at any time and therefore there cannot be a liability unless an announcement has been made

It is possible that a past record in relation to dividends could create a constructive obligation under IAS 37 but there would still need to be some action such as a proposal of a dividend by the end of the reporting period – otherwise, it is treated under IAS 10 and therefore not recognised

If the proposed dividend was approved before the financial statements were authorised to issue, it should still be disclosed in the notes to the financial statements even though it is not recognised

Fair Value – IFRS 13

Suggested mark allocation in an FR question (CR Q2): 6 marks (relatively new topic and complex)

Definition under IFRS 13

The price that would be received to sell an asset or paid to transfer a liability in an orderly transaction between market participants at the measurement date

IFRS 13 does not apply (either in relation to **measurement** nor to **disclosures**) to

Share-based payment transactions within the scope of IFRS 2

Leasing transactions within the scope of IAS 17

Net realisable value under IAS 2

IFRS 13 **disclosure** requirements do not apply to

Plan assets measured at FV in accordance with IAS 19

Plan investments measured at FV in accordance with IAS 26

Assets for which the recoverable amount is FV less disposal costs under IAS 36

Measurement

It is assumed that the transaction would take place in the principal market or in the most advantageous market, in an orderly transaction rather than under a forced sale

FV is not adjusted for transaction costs but these can be taken into account when determining the most advantageous market

Non-financial assets are valued based on the use to which the asset can be put in its highest and best use

The use of bid prices for financial assets and the use of ask prices for financial liabilities is permitted, but not required – IFRS 13 does not preclude the use of mid-market pricing

Example measurement methods for liabilities and own equity instruments

Quoted price exists for an **identical or similar** liability/own equity instrument – use the **quoted** price

No quoted price exists for the transfer of an **identical or similar** liability/own equity instrument but there is an **identical item held by another entity as an asset** – measure the fair value of the liability or equity instrument from the **perspective of a market participant that holds the identical item as an asset** at the measurement date

No quoted price exists for the transfer of an **identical or similar** liability/own equity instrument and there is **no identical item held by another entity as an asset** – measure the fair value of the liability or equity instrument using a **valuation technique from the perspective of a market participant** that owes the liability or has issued the equity

IFRS 13 levels

Level 1   quoted prices in an active market for identical assets or liabilities

Level 2   inputs other than Level 1 that are observable, either directly or indirectly

              e.g. quoted prices for similar assets in active markets or for identical or similar assets in non-active markets or use of quoted interest rates for valuation purposes

Level 3   unobservable inputs for the asset or liability

              e.g. the entity's own assumptions about market exit value

The entity should **maximise** the use of **observable** inputs and **minimise** the use of **unobservable** inputs

Valuation approaches

Income approach   discounted future flows (cash flows, income and expenses)

Market approach   use of prices and other relevant information generated by market transactions involving identical or comparable assets, liabilities or a group of assets and liabilities (such as a business)

Cost approach   the amount that would be required currently to replace the service capacity of an asset (current replacement cost)

The valuation of unlisted equity shares is likely to be particularly challenging and will almost certainly be classified as a Level 3 measurement due to the use of unobservable inputs

Entities may use more than one valuation technique to measure FV in a given situation – a change of valuation technique is considered to be a change of accounting estimate in accordance with IAS 8 and must be disclosed in the financial statements

An asset-based approach would be more relevant to a property business whilst an income approach would be more relevant to a service business

Examples of inputs used to measure FV

Level 1	Equity shares (listed)	Market price (unadjusted quoted price)
Level 2	Licensing arrangement	Royalty rate in contract
	CGU	Valuation multiple from comparable businesses
	Inventory	Comparable items, adjusted for relevant differences
	Building	Price per square metre from observable market data
Level 3	CGU	Forecast from entity's own data
	Share option (other than employee-held)	Volatility and related valuation model
	Interest rate swap	Adjustment to mid-market consensus valuation using data not directly observable or as corroborated by observable market data

Financial instruments – AFS asset

Suggested mark allocation in an FR question (CR Q2): 4 marks

Initial recognition should be at **fair value** (**cost** of the investment)

Transaction costs should be **capitalised** into the value of the asset – do not expense the transaction costs

Update at each year end to fair value – use the lower or "bid" price if you are given a bid-offer spread quotation

On sale, recycle any accumulated gains or losses held in the AFS reserve into the P&L – the AFS reserve entries on the item must be fully cleared out on sale

Do not forget to check for a gain in the **current** year as well – this will not be in the AFS reserve **brought forward** but forms part of the total gain or loss

The total gain or loss should (assuming no impairment) be **sales proceeds** less the **originally recognised amount** – this gain or loss will be a mixture of amounts in the **AFS reserve** from prior years and the **current year** gain/loss

Recognition at cost

It may be difficult to estimate the FV of instruments such as unquoted equity – in this case the instrument should be recorded at **cost** and no gain should arise on their subsequent measurement

Exchange differences

A gain or loss on an AFS asset should be recognised in OCI except for impairment losses and **forex gains and losses (IAS 39 para 55(b)**

However, for **AFS assets that are not monetary items** (for example **equity instruments**) the gain or loss that is recognised in OCI **includes any related foreign currency exchange component** (IAS 39 para AG83)

Financial instruments – convertible bonds

Suggested mark allocation in an FR question (CR Q2): 6 marks

A convertible bond is a compound instrument per IAS 32 – the equity and liability components should be separated

The liability component at inception is calculated as the present value of future cash flows (capital and interest) from the instruments, discounted by a market interest rate for an instrument with the same terms and conditions **except for** the ability to convert to shares

Note – do **not** use the **coupon** rate involved in the instrument for the discounting – use a **market rate** for an equivalent instrument without the conversion option

The **equity** component is the **residual** amount i.e. the difference between the calculated liability and the consideration paid for the bond

Pro forma – example of a £20m loan at 5% with a discount factor of 7% (rate applicable to a similar instrument without the conversion option)

	Cash flow at 5%	Discount at 7%	£000
31 Dec 2015	1,000	$1/1.07$	935
31 Dec 2016	1,000	$1/1.07^2$	873
31 Dec 2017	1,000	$1/1.07^3$	816
31 Dec 2018	1,000*	$1/1.07^4$	763
	20,000*	$1/1.07^4$	15,258
Total liability			18,645
Equity (balance)			1,355
Consideration			20,000

The cash flow is calculated by multiplying the consideration by the applicable coupon interest rate i.e. the rate applying to the loan. These figures are all based on amounts **before** you do the split accounting.

*As the capital repayment and final year of interest are discounted by the same discount factor, you may wish to do the final 2 rows above as a single calculation to save time (i.e. 21,000 at $1/1.07^4$)

Note that it is possible to use an **annuity factor** for the **interest** cash flows as these are the same each year – this may save time if you have an instrument that lasts for a few years

However, if you use an **annuity factor** for the **interest** cash flows, do not forget to also have a **separate discount factor** calculation for the large **capital** repayment in the final year

Treatment of transaction costs

The total transaction costs should be split **pro rata** between the liability and equity components based on the pro forma calculation above i.e. you must find the PV of the liability and the residual equity amount before allocating the transaction costs – do not forget to **reduce** the value of the **liability** and the **equity** component by the allocated transaction costs

Financial instruments – HTM

Suggested mark allocation in an FR question (CR Q2): 4 marks

Carried at **amortised cost**

Pro forma (assuming interest is paid in cash at the end of the reporting period)

Opening balance

Plus interest at EIR (P&L)

Less cash paid at coupon rate (SCF)

Closing balance

Disposal

Remember to **update** the amortised cost **through to the date of disposal** i.e. allow for any interest accrued during the year of an HTM asset sold partway through the year – **usually** the instrument will have its **cash payment at the year-end** so if there is disposal part way through the year you will be adding some interest but not deducting anything for a payment received

Tainting rule

The disposal of a significant proportion of a HTM asset before maturity results in all assets in the HTM category becoming **tainted** for **2 years**

Any remaining assets in the HTM category must be transferred to the **AFS** category

The entity may not use the HTM category for **2 years**

The penalty applies **unless** the amount reclassified/sold is insignificant to the total amount of HTM investments **or** the sale was within 3 months of maturity **or** after the entity has collected substantially all the amounts of the original principal, **or** was the result of an event beyond the entity's control and which could not reasonably have been anticipated

Financial instruments – the 5 types – treatment

5 types?

Please note that this is not a mistake – in addition to the categories of FVtPL, AFS, HTM and L&R there is also the category of equity instruments held at **cost** due to the lack of a reliable method of estimating fair value – this final category does not tend to be tested very often but just to remind you!

Related party?

Look carefully at the percentage held – is the examiner suggesting that there could also be a related party transaction via a holding which qualifies as an associate?

If the holding is low at around 5% then it is unlikely that an associate relationship exists

Summary of treatment of financial instrument categories

Category	Description	Measurement after initial recognition	Gains and losses
FVtPL	Held for sale in the short term (held for trading) Or designated under this heading ("fair value option")	FV	In profit or loss
AFS	Non-derivatives designated as AFS or not classified under any of the other 3 headings	FV	In OCI but recognise investment income, impairment losses and forex gains and losses in profit or loss
L&R	Non-derivatives with fixed or determinable payments that are not quoted in an active market, not designated at FVtPL, not held for trading or designated as available for sale	Amortised cost	In profit or loss
HTM	Non-derivatives with fixed or determinable payments and fixed maturity with a positive intention to hold to maturity and not designated under any of the other 3 headings	Amortised cost	In profit or loss

Derecognition

Derecognition should occur when the contractual rights to the cash flows from the financial asset expire or the entity transfers substantially all the risks and rewards of ownership of the financial asset to another party

FVtPL

Must be held with the intention of **short-term trading** for profit

Also includes **all derivatives** unless part of a designated hedge

Transaction costs should be **expensed** through the P&L – note that this is a **different** treatment to the other financial assets discussed below

If the item is quoted on a bid-offer spread basis (e.g. £5.03-£5.06) then treat the difference (here £0.03) as a **transaction cost** and immediately **expense** this, using the **lower** figure for the purposes of the capitalised amount

Note that the client accountant may have **expensed** the transaction costs through **finance charges** but it may be more appropriate to reclassify these to **operating** costs as they do not relate to interest charges but rather professional fees

Re-measure the **asset** at the year end to **the fair value** and take the gain or loss directly **to profit or loss**, remembering to adjust the **value** of the asset with an appropriate **credit** or **debit** as the other side of the transaction on the SFP

Note that IAS 39 does **not** state **where** in the P&L the gain or loss should be recorded but many companies would treat a gain as **operating income** or **other income**

AFS

Recognise at **fair value** and capitalise transaction costs i.e. increase the size of the asset by the transaction costs (do not expense the transaction costs in the P&L) – however, **ignore** transaction costs when calculating the **year end fair value** – only consider transaction costs at inception

If the AFS asset is denominated in a **foreign currency**, the fair value at the year-end must be calculated using the **closing rate** – this is a change from the normal treatment for a non-monetary asset

Use the lower (sale) price if a bid offer spread (e.g. £4.50-£4.75) is provided for the purposes of the year end estimate

Ignore **transaction costs** when calculating the **year-end** fair value – these are not relevant as we are not actually disposing of the asset – we are simply **revaluing** it

Take the gain or loss at the year end through **OCI** and store in the **AFS reserve**, unless there is evidence of a **permanent impairment** in which case the loss is taken to profit or loss **immediately**

Remember to increase or decrease the value of the AFS asset with an appropriate **debit** or **credit** as the other side of the gain for the SFP

Recognition at cost

It may be difficult to estimate the FV of instruments such as unquoted equity – in this case the instrument should be recorded at **cost** and no gain should arise on subsequent measurement

This is a **last resort**, particularly for assets which otherwise would be at FV so it should not be used unless necessary

Exchange or modification of debt

When a new loan is agreed, the treatment depends on whether the new terms are **substantially different** from the old terms

The terms are **substantially different** if the PV of the cash flows under the new terms including any fees payable/receivable, discounted at the original EIR, is **10% or more different** from the PV of the remaining cash flows under the original terms

If there is a **difference of 10% or more** then there is an "**extinguishment**" of the old liability – the difference between the carrying amount extinguished and the consideration paid should be recognised in profit or loss – fees payable/receivable should be recognised as part of that gain or loss

If there is a **difference of less than 10%** then there is a "**modification**" of the terms – the existing liability is not derecognised and its carrying amount is simply adjusted by the fees payable/receivable and amortised over the remaining term of the modified liability

Transaction costs

These should be **added** to the initial FV (or deducted in the case of liabilities) except in the case of financial assets or liabilities classified at **FVtPL** where transaction costs should be **expensed**

However, transaction costs that would be incurred on disposal are not considered at subsequent re-measurement of financial instruments

A useful rule is to remember to always debit transaction costs (increase an asset, reduce a liability) – after all, the credit side would have to be to cash or payables

This treatment will affect the EIR applied to assets or liabilities carried at amortised cost – it should be built into a correctly calculated EIR

If a bid-offer spread is quoted then IAS 39 treats the spread as a transaction cost so if the asset is at FVtPL the difference should be **expensed** – for other assets, the spread is immediately added into the initial cost so effectively the entity capitalises the higher figure of the bid-offer spread (if an asset is quoted at £75-£78 then for all categories other than FVtPL we can effectively use the **£78** price for initial recognition purposes – the spread of £3 is still a transaction cost but it is added back to the £75 to create the initial recognition amount so simply use £78)

Reclassification of financial assets

Under the original IAS 39 it was possible to reclassify all financial assets other than assets at FVtPL – however, see the amendment below.

Remember that reclassification of HTM assets carries a penalty under the "tainting rules"

Reclassification out of FVtPL

Following a 2008 amendment IAS 39, reclassification out of the FVtPL category is now allowed in restricted circumstances if circumstances have changed and the intention is now to hold the assets for their investment potential – the amendment is effective retrospectively from 1 July 2008

The amendment only applies to some non-derivative assets – reclassification is not allowed for any financial liabilities at FVtPL, any derivatives or any financial assets that were designated at FVtPL on initial recognition under the "fair value option"

The amendment therefore only relates to debt and equity financial assets

The amendment does not allow reclassification **into** FVtPL

Additional disclosures are required, showing the amounts reclassified in and out of each category, the FV of reclassified assets, FV gains or losses recognised in the period of reclassification and any new EIR

If a debt instrument would have met the L&R criteria if not required to be classified as held for trading at recognition then it may be reclassified out of FVtPL provided that the entity has the intention and ability to hold the asset for the foreseeable future or until maturity

If a debt instrument was classified as AFS but would have met the L&R criteria, it may be reclassified to L&R provided that the entity has the intention and ability to hold the asset for the foreseeable future or until maturity

Other debt instruments or any equity instrument may be reclassified from FVtPL to AFS (or for debt only, from FVtPL to HTM) if the asset is no longer held for selling in the short term

Reclassified assets are remeasured to FV at the date of reclassification – previously recognised gains and losses cannot be reversed – FV at the date of reclassification becomes the new cost or amortised cost of the financial asset

The normal IAS 39 rules apply – for amortised cost assets, a new EIR will be determined – for assets classified out of AFS, amounts previously recognised in OCI must be reclassified to profit or loss

However for reclassified debt instruments, if the entity increases its estimate of the recoverability of future cash flows the carrying amount is not adjusted upwards (as would be the case under IAS 39) but instead a new effective interest rate must be applied from that date on, allowing the increase in recoverability of cash flows to be recognised over the expected life of the financial asset

Financial instruments – loan impairment

Suggested mark allocation in an FR question (CR Q2): 3 marks

A loan asset will often be carried at **amortised cost**

Pro forma

Opening balance

Plus interest at EIR (P&L)

Less cash paid at coupon rate (SCF)

Closing balance

If there is evidence of impairment you should calculate the expected carrying amount before impairment as normal – then compare this to the present value of cash flows discounted under the **original** Effective Interest Rate – do not use a more up-to-date market interest rate as this would **impose a fair value approach** on an instrument correctly held at **amortised cost**

The difference between these 2 figures is the **impairment** and this should be taken to **profit or loss**

Note that you should always use the original Effective Interest Rate and not any other interest rates that the examiner might include in the data – this is because switching the rate to a market rate would impose a fair value approach but this should not be applied to assets held at amortised cost (unlike the FVtPL or AFS categories, amortised cost does not use a fair value approach).

Future accounting periods – IFRS 9

Note – do not write too much on IFRS 9 as IAS 39 remains the main standard applicable to the examination

IFRS 9 will implement an "expected loss" model which may lead to earlier recognition of impairment than under IAS 39's "incurred loss" model – under IFRS 9, it is not necessary to wait for an impairment event to occur

The initial credit loss allowance/provision will be equal to the expected loss in the next 12 months (probability of default x total lifetime expected credit losses from the default)

If credit risk increases significantly since initial recognition then the credit loss/allowance is replaced by lifetime expected credit losses (the 3 stage model)

Financial instruments – Loans & Receivables

Suggested mark allocation in an FR question (CR Q2): 3 marks

Carried at **amortised cost**

Pro forma

Opening balance

Plus interest at EIR (P&L)

Less cash paid at coupon rate (SCF)

Closing balance

Trade receivables

IAS 39 classifies trade receivables as financial assets within the L&R category

Such assets should be measured at **amortised cost** using the Effective Interest Rate method

However, short-term receivables with no stated interest rates can be measured at the original invoice amount, if the effect of discounting is **not material**

The entity should consider on an **annual basis** whether there is **objective evidence** that the receivable is **impaired** – if so, the carrying amount of the receivable must be compared with the present value of the estimated future cash flows, discounted using the original Effective Interest Rate

The calculation of impairments must **not** use a **formulaic approach** such as a **general allowance** based on past experience as this is unlikely to be an accurate estimate of the cash flows – this is only acceptable if it produces an estimate sufficiently close to that produced by the more specific IAS 39 method which looks at discounted cash flows

Future accounting periods – IFRS 9

Note – do not write too much on IFRS 9 as IAS 39 remains the main standard applicable to the examination

IFRS 9 will implement an "expected loss" model which may lead to earlier recognition of impairment than under IAS 39's "incurred loss" model – under IFRS 9, it is not necessary to wait for an impairment event to occur

The initial credit loss allowance/provision will be equal to the expected loss in the next 12 months (probability of default x total lifetime expected credit losses from the default)

If credit risk increases significantly since initial recognition then the credit loss/allowance is replaced by lifetime expected credit losses (the 3 stage model)

However, for trade receivables that do not have an IAS 18/IFRS 15 financing element, the loss allowance is measured as the lifetime expected credit losses from initial recognition (simplified approach)

Forex translation – single entity accounts

Suggested mark allocation in an FR question (CR Q2): 2 marks per issue

(Please note that this topic covers currency recognition rules for a single company rather than the consolidation of an overseas subsidiary into the group accounts – for the more complex issue of consolidation of an overseas subsidiary please see the section starting on page 84.)

IAS 21 requires amounts to be translated into the entity's "functional currency"

The **functional currency** is "the currency of the primary economic environment in which the entity operates"

The **primary economic environment** "is normally the one in which it primarily generates and expends cash"

Translation rules – single entity accounts (see exceptions in the next section)

Initial recognition – use the **spot rate** on the date of the transaction – an average rate may be used if exchange rates do not fluctuate significantly

Monetary items – use the **closing rate**

Non-monetary items carried at **historical cost** – use the exchange rate at the date of the transaction (historical rate)

Non-monetary items carried at FV (including AFS assets) – use the exchange rate that existed **when the value was measured (closing rate)**

Exchange differences should be recognised such as to match the underlying transaction – exchange differences on monetary items should be recognised in the P&L – exchange differences on non-monetary items recognised in OCI should also be recognised through OCI

Exceptions to the general rules

A monetary item designed as a hedge of a net investment – any exchange difference that forms part of the gain or loss on the hedging instrument is recognised as **OCI**

A monetary item designated as a hedging instrument in a cash flow hedge – any exchange difference that forms part of the gain or loss on the hedging instrument is recognised as **OCI**

Exchange differences arising in respect of monetary items which are part of the net investment are recognised in profit or loss in the individual financial statements – however, in the CSFP the exchange differences are recognised **through OCI and within equity**

Normally non-monetary items are not retranslated at the year-end in the individual entity accounts so no exchange differences arise – however, note the following exceptions:

When a gain or loss on a non-monetary item is recognised in OCI (e.g. a property denominated in a foreign currency is revalued or an AFS asset which is an equity instrument) then any related exchange differences should be recognised as OCI

When a gain or loss on a non-monetary item is recognised in profit or loss, any exchange component of that gain or loss is also recognised in profit or loss

Remember that in the impairment testing of foreign currency non-monetary assets, the carrying amount should be reset to the lower of the carrying amount translated at the exchange rate at the date when that amount was determined (i.e. an historic rate at a past date) and the recoverable amount, translated at the exchange rate at the date when that value was determined (e.g. the **closing rate** at the reporting date)

Inventories

Inventories are a **non-monetary** asset – the inventory (and associated liability if not yet paid in cash) are recorded at the spot rate on the day of purchase

The inventories need no further translating – any **liability** to pay for the inventories, however, **is** a **monetary** item and should be translated at the reporting date using the **closing rate** with exchange gains and losses being taken to **profit or loss**

Inventories must be valued at the **lower** of cost and net realisable value

Going Concern

Suggested mark allocation in an FR question (CR Q2): 2 marks

Duties of management and disclosures

Directors are **required** to report that the business is a going concern, with assumptions or qualifications if necessary – if the company has a full listing then this will be part of their responsibilities under the **UK Corporate Governance Code**

If there is adequate **disclosure** in the financial statements by the directors regarding the uncertainties of the going concern assumption then an **unmodified** audit opinion with an **emphasis of matter** paragraph is likely to be sufficient

If the directors **do not disclose** going concern uncertainties appropriately then it may be necessary to **modify** the audit opinion

Duties of auditors

Discuss with management and perform other audit tests

Government Grants

Suggested mark allocation in an FR question (CR Q2): 6 marks

Recognition

Recognition of a government grant should occur when there is reasonable assurance that

> the entity will comply with the relevant conditions and

> the entity will receive the grant

Make sure you apply these points to the scenario by checking if the conditions have been complied with (referencing the relevant facts in your answer)

The likely mistake made by the client is to use a cash basis rather than an accruals basis to recognise the grant

Capital grants

There are 2 methods of recognition – these are both designed to ensure that the grant hits the P&L at the same time/rate as the underlying item on which a grant has been given

Note that both methods give the same net P&L impact so there is no "favourable" approach (although the impact on certain ratios may be different)

Netting off method

Deduct the amount of the grant from the cost of the asset – this will reduce the amount which is depreciated, reducing the depreciation charge

> However, it will also reduce the value of assets, which could impact on ratios

Deferred income method

Set up the grant as deferred income in the SFP – release this to the P&L on a systematic and rational basis over the useful life of the asset (normally this would correspond to the method of depreciation on the related asset)

> This will leave the asset value at a higher amount, impacting ratios – however, the deferred income will increase liabilities

Income grants

e.g. grants to employ local employees over a 3 year period

Such a grant should be recognised over the same period as the underlying item i.e. 3 years in the example here

The grant should not be recognised unless there is reasonable assurance that the entity will comply with any **conditions** attached to the grant and that the **grant will be received**

Note in some cases the second criterion will be fulfilled automatically as the money will already have been received – you will therefore only have to assess the first criterion based on the **probability** of fulfilment of conditions

It is likely that the client will have recognised the **cash** received as the P&L entry – this is incorrect – you will therefore have to set up a **deferred income** account as some revenue may not be recognised yet

The grant should **not** be recognised as **revenue** – it could either be shown as other income in the P&L or it could be netted off against the expenditure to which it relates e.g. as part of operating costs

Make sure you split the deferred income account into current and non-current elements

As it is likely that you will have some **time apportionment** the current year, it is easiest to first calculate a full year of revenue as you can use this instantly as the current element of the deferred income account – then time apportion this full year figure as appropriate for the current year to provide the P&L amount – the remainder must be the non-current element of deferred income

Summary of technique

1. Calculate a full year of deferred income – current liability

2. Time apportion the above figure from step 1 as required – current year P&L income

3. The remaining balance (i.e. the total grant figure minus figures from step 1 in step 2) is the non-current liability

Repayment of government grants

If a grant becomes repayable then this should be accounted for as a change in accounting estimate

Repayment of an income grant

This should be first set against any unamortised deferred credit set up in respect of the grant – to the extent that repayment exceeds any such deferred credit or where no deferred credit exists then the repayment should be recognised immediately as an expense

Repayment of a capital grant

This should be recognised either by increasing the carrying amount of the asset or reducing the deferred income balance by the amount repayable

The cumulative additional depreciation that would have been recognised to date as an expense in the absence of the grant should be recognised immediately as an expense

Disclosures

Accounting policy adopted for government grants, including the methods of presentation

Nature and extent of government grants recognised in the financial statements

Indication of other forms of government assistance from which the entity has directly benefited

Unfulfilled conditions and other contingencies attaching to government assistance that have been recognised

Groups – acquisitions

Suggested mark allocation in an FR question (CR Q2): 7-8 marks

Tip

Do not forget to talk about the NCI!

We have provided several further Group sections on the following pages so please do make use of these

Loss-making subsidiary – in this case, there will probably be a mark for suggesting that an impairment review is needed even in the year of acquisition

Treatment

Consolidation should occur if there is "**control**" over the subsidiary

A **majority shareholding** i.e. greater than 50% would **normally** indicate control – however, other factors may be relevant under IFRS 10 (see next page)

Issues to consider

Measure consideration at FV

Transaction costs such as professional fees should not form part of the consideration and should instead be recognised directly in profit or loss

> An exception (rarely tested) is that the costs of arranging financial liabilities (e.g. loans) and issuing equity are deducted from the liability/equity

Intangible assets should be recognised separately if they arise from legal or other contractual rights – these assets do not form part of goodwill – they should be amortised – there will be an NCI impact

Goodwill should be reviewed annually for impairment

Gain on a bargain purchase (negative goodwill)

Here the value of assets acquired exceeds the consideration paid

Reassess the identification and measurement of the net assets and the measurement of the consideration

If the amounts are correct then the gain on bargain purchase should be recognised as part of profit or loss for the period

Tip – do not forget to mention the NCI impact of your adjustments – easy additional marks on a follow through approach for a relatively simple calculation

We have provided several further Group sections on the following pages so please do make use of these

Assessing control under IFRS 10 – advanced points

Note – only include these points if the matter of control appears complicated in the scenario – in most group answers, you would not need the below details

IFRS 10 states that an investor controls and investee if and only if it has all the following

> power over the investee

> exposure, or rights, to variable returns from its involvement with the investee

> the ability to use its power over the investee to affect the amount of the investor's returns

The fact that board members may not have actually exercised control in practice is not a determining factor in deciding whether the entity has control over the investee

We also need to consider powers to appoint board members – if there are such appointment powers for board members other than the entity which has a majority shareholding, then the matter may not be so straightforward and the shareholding greater than 50% may not be sufficient to create "control"

In some cases, control of board decisions over a fundamental aspect of the company such as R&D or finance e.g. if the owner can appoint a specific Director to be the head of R&D or Finance could also confer control if that division is fundamental to the investee

The right to acquire further shares through a call option could also be relevant – IFRS 10 requires an investor to consider potential voting rights in considering whether it has control and whether they are substantive i.e. whether the holder has the practical ability to exercise the right

If "control" is not held, the investment cannot be recognised as a subsidiary and would be recognised instead as an associate

Groups – associates

Suggested mark allocation in an FR question (CR Q2): 3 marks

A holding of 20% or more of the voting power in an investee is presumed to provide significant influence and create an associate position – however, the 20% figure is rebuttable and an associate could exist with more or less than this amount depending on whether the facts indicate that significant influence exists through one or more of the following

> representation on the board of directors or participation in policy making decisions
>
> material transactions between the investor and investee
>
> interchange of managerial personnel
>
> provision of essential technical information

Equity method of accounting

Recognise initially at cost – increase or decrease by the investor's share in the post-acquisition change in the associate's net assets (profits or losses)

Cost	X
Share of post-acquisition change in net assets	X
Less investor's **share** of dividends paid by associate	(X)
Less impairment losses to date	(X)
	X

The investor's share in profits/losses should be recognised in the investor's CSPL net of any impairment loss

Eliminate profits and losses on transactions between the investor and associate to the extent of the investor's share

The investor's interest can only be written below nil (creating a liability) if the investor has incurred obligations on behalf of the associate

There is **no line by line addition** of items in the SFP – instead there is a single line under non-current assets

No goodwill calculation is performed

The whole interest is subject to an **impairment review** if there is an objective **indicator of impairment**

Trading transactions should not be cancelled on consolidation – the associate is not part of the group

> No adjustment to revenue or CoS in the CSPL
>
> Receivables and payables due to/from the associate should be carried across into the CSFP

Unrealised profits should be eliminated, but only to the extent of the investor's share – the adjustment is made in the books of the seller

> This applies to both the transfer of goods and the transfer of non-current assets

Groups – associate to subsidiary

Suggested mark allocation in an FR question (CR Q2): 7-8 marks

Key points to mention

Refer to the fact that control has been achieved – goodwill arises on the transaction and an NCI will be created in relation to the percentage owned by minority shareholders

Treatment

Continue to treat the entity as an associate right up to the date when control is achieved – therefore continue to apply the equity method and credit or debit the statement of profit or loss with a time apportioned amount of profit or loss e.g. £5m x 4 / 12 x 30%

> If this is a profit, the debit would increase the investment in associates in the SFP

State that for the remaining months of the year after control is achieved, the entity should be consolidated using the acquisition method and assets, liabilities, income and expenses should be fully consolidated in

Consider whether there is an NCI – if the entity is now 100% owned, state that there are no entries in respect of NCI – if the entity is now, say 80% owned, then state that the NCI will hold 20% of assets and will take 20% of profit or loss for the period after control is achieved

Calculate the gain on the increase in stake (in the exam, it is highly likely that the entity will record a gain and not a loss here) using the following pro forma

Original cost	X
Cumulative share of profit or loss to the end of the previous period	X
Share of profit or loss for the current period to the date control is achieved	X*
Carrying amount at time of change in status	X**

*this figure should be the same amount that you calculated above when indicating the amount of profit or loss to take **before** control is achieved

**State that IFRS 3 requires this carrying amount to be restated to fair value – hence compare the total of the above pro-forma calculation with the FV of the shares given in the question – if the FV is higher than the carrying amount calculated above, a gain occurs

In an exam scenario, it is likely that there will be a **gain** as the FV of the shares is normally higher than the carrying amount in the above pro forma – state that this gain is recognised in **profit or loss for the year**, most likely within "other operating income"

AFS investment

Any gains or losses on the AFS investment previously taken through OCI into the AFS reserve should now be transferred to profit or loss – this amount relates to gains or losses in years prior to the acquisition

Re-measure to fair value immediately prior to acquisition – this could add a **further** gain or loss in the current year to be added to the cost of investment and taken to profit or loss

Goodwill calculation

As well as calculating the gain on sale as a result of updating to FV (see above) you will need to calculate goodwill as normal as a subsidiary has been acquired

The only real difference is that you need to include the **FV of the shares** in **addition** to the normal inclusion of **consideration** – in other words at the top of the pro forma you should have the **consideration** (as normal) **plus the FV of the shares acquired** when transforming the associate into a subsidiary (different to the normal calculation)

The rest of the goodwill calculation is as normal – do not forget to mention that the goodwill should not be impaired but should be reviewed for impairment on an annual basis (and earlier if there is any specific indicator of impairment)

Groups – disposal of a subsidiary

Suggested mark allocation in an FR question (CR Q2): 6 marks

Complete disposal

Overview of the complete disposal calculation

Effectively, you are comparing the proceeds received against the value of the subsidiary which the entity holds (net assets less the NCI plus remaining goodwill after impairment)

Rather than trying to calculate all of this in one big calculation as the Study Manual and past papers try to do, we would recommend that you split the calculation into 3 parts:

1. Remaining value of goodwill – goodwill at acquisition less impairments to date

2. Carrying amount of net assets based disposal – net assets at the prior year end plus or minus profit or loss for the current year (look out the time apportionment here)

3. NCI in net assets at the date of disposal – this may be tricky but just make an attempt and take the follow-through marks

After calculating the 3 elements, you can put together a final working as

Proceeds	X
plus NCI at disposal	X
less total subsidiary net assets at disposal	(X)
less goodwill at disposal	(X)
Profit or loss on disposal	X/(X)

(NCI is added back to ensure that on a net basis only the parent's share of the subsidiary's net assets is being disposed of)

The profit or loss on disposal should be recognised in the CSPL under discontinued operations

The results for the subsidiary up to the date of disposal should be included in the CSPL

The parent no longer controls any of the assets or liabilities of the subsidiary after sale so mention that the CSFP should not recognise any of the subsidiary's assets or liabilities

The NCI should include the NCI share of the results of the subsidiary up to the date of disposal (look out for time apportionment here) – on disposal, the CSoCIE should have the remaining NCI deducted to clear out the NCI after disposal

Tip – consider IFRS 5

If the investment in the subsidiary represented a separate major line of business of the group, the results of the subsidiary for the year should be presented separately in accordance with IFRS 5

A single net figure for the profit or loss for the discontinued operation should be disclosed on the face of the CSPL – this is made up of the profit or loss on disposal and the profit or loss for the period to the date of disposal

A disclosure note should show the breakdown of this figure into revenue, costs and profit on disposal

The prior period results should be reclassified as discontinued in order to ensure comparability

Groups – forex consolidation

Suggested mark allocation in an FR question (CR Q2): 20 marks if no other elements of the question – 8 marks if only a "mini consolidation" is required i.e. there are several other FR points in the question

Note that there will be plenty of marks allocated to **explaining the principles** behind the adjustments – you must include **some narrative** and not just the numbers

Important note

We strongly recommend that you take in a copy of a past paper or Question Bank example of a full forex consolidation, annotated with your own reminders and notes – this will be helpful to follow the process through

This section provides reminders only of how to perform the process – it does not provide a fully worked-through example and we do not know what particular areas you find difficult so please do create your own personally-annotated example and bring this into the examination with you.

Treatment

Functional currency

This is the currency of the primary **economic operations** of the entity

Presentation currency

This is the currency in which the financial statements are **presented**

The presentation currency of the parent of the group is likely to be the same as the functional currency

Overview of the forex consolidation process (see next pages for the details of each step)

The financial statements of subsidiaries with a functional currency other than the presentation currency of the parent must be translated on consolidation.

1. Translate **assets** and **liabilities** at the **closing** rate at the year end

2. Translate **equity** on acquisition at **either** the exchange rate **at acquisition** or the **closing** rate

(Per the Study Manual, no guidance is provided in IAS 21 as to how amounts in equity should be translated – therefore **either** approach is permissible although an entity should follow a **consistent** policy between periods)

3. Translate **income** and **expenses** at the **average** rate for the year

Previously the financial statements balanced but now you have (correctly) started using different exchange rates so an imbalance necessarily occurs – therefore:

4. Present in a **separate component** of equity the exchange differences which inevitably arise from application of the above rules – these **exchange differences** are reported through OCI rather than the P&L

5. Treat **goodwill** as an **asset** of the relevant subsidiary and translate at the **closing rate**

6. Eliminate **intragroup** balances and transactions as **normal** on consolidation

Steps 1 & 2 – Translation of SFP

Translate assets and liabilities at the **closing** rate

Translate **equity** and **pre-acquisition** retained earnings at the rate applicable on acquisition or at the closing rate (the Study Manual states that either method is acceptable, provided that it is applied consistently from one period to the next)

Translate **post-acquisition** retained earnings at the **average** rates for the current year

To make the statements balance, set up a **translation reserve** as necessary and record this immediately below retained earnings in the SFP

> You can enter this simply as a balancing figure but ideally it should match the amount calculated in the **Translation reserve in the SFP section** below – try to use the result of that below calculation if possible because it is simpler than getting all the above changes correct

Step 3 – Translation of SPLOCI

Translate all amounts at the **average** rate for the year

As all amounts are translated at the **same** rate, there is **no need for any translation reserve** for the P&L

However, there may of course be some exchange gains and losses on items such as **loans** or **intra-company purchases** as a result of fluctuating exchange rates during the year – these are included in the SPLOCI and are translated at the average rate as with any other items in the SPLOCI

The point is that you do not need to set up a special "consolidation only" item in relation to the consolidation process of the P&L and OCI (unlike with the SFP and goodwill)

Step 4 – Translation reserve in the SFP (confirmation of subsidiary translation reserve and creation of Consolidated translation reserve)

1. Translate **opening** net assets at the **closing** rate and compare these with **opening** net assets at the **opening** rate

2. Translate profits at the **closing** rate and compare these with profits at the **average** rate

Pro forma

Opening net assets at opening rate

Opening net assets at closing rate

X

Profit/loss at the average rate

Profit/loss at the closing rate

X

Exchange gain or loss (net of above 2 totals)   X

3. The net impact of the above 2 translations may lead to a gain or loss – this amount is included as the **translation reserve** of the **subsidiary** and should be the same figure as the translation reserve created as a balancing figure when translating the subsidiary's SFP (see previous page)

> We would recommend that you use the figure based on the working above to put into your SFP rather than simply using a balancing amount as discussed on the previous page because then you should get the relevant marks for this part of the Translation reserve – if you just use a balancing approach, an error in another area of the SFP will mean that you lose this mark as well

4. Allocate the above net gain or net loss to the **group** based on its ownership percentage – allocate the balance to the NCI

5. Finally add or deduct the exchange gain or loss on re-translation of **goodwill** (see below)

6. Add together the group share of the net gain or net loss from step 4 to the gain or loss on retranslation of goodwill from step 5 – this figure is included in the **Consolidated SFP** as a **translation reserve** and is recognised through OCI, not through the P&L

Step 5 – Translation of goodwill

Set up the normal pro forma to calculate goodwill, including consideration transferred as compared to the FV of net assets acquired

Remember to split this between the group and NCI

Translate these amounts at the exchange rate applicable at the **date of acquisition**

Allocate any impairment losses, remembering to split these between the group and NCI – translate the **impairment losses** at the **closing rate** at the year end

Translate the year-end figures after impairment at the **closing rate**

As a result of applying different exchange rates within the pro forma you will need to set up a **foreign exchange gain or loss** to force the figures to agree to back to the value of the goodwill at the year-end as translated into domestic currency

Translation reserve and impact on the CSPLOCI

Opening and closing net assets and profits should be translated based on the same principles as above for the SFP

1. Translate opening net assets at the closing rate and compare these with opening net assets at the opening rate

2. Translate profits at the closing rate and compare this with profits at the average rate

The net impact of the above 2 translations may lead to a gain or loss

This amount forms part of the Exchange differences on translating foreign operations through OCI in the CSPLOCI – note that the NCI should take its share of this as part of the NCI figure in the CSPLOCI

The gain or loss on retranslation of goodwill forms the second part of the Exchange differences on translating foreign operations under OCI in the CSPLOCI – this is calculated as above

Set up the normal pro forma to calculate goodwill, including consideration transferred as compared to the FV of net assets acquired

Remember to split this between the group and NCI

Translate these amounts at the exchange rate applicable at the **date of acquisition**

Allocate any **impairment losses**, remembering to split these between the group and NCI – translate the impairment losses at the **closing rate** at the year end

Translate the goodwill figure **after** impairment at the **closing rate** at the year end

As a result of applying 2 different exchange rates in the pro forma (acquisition rate in the top-half of the pro forma and closing rate in the bottom half of the pro forma) you will need to set up a foreign exchange gain or loss to **force the figures to agree to the bottom row, based on the closing rate**

Note that the NCI should also take its share of this as part of the NCI figure in the CSPLOCI – this should be recorded at the bottom of the CSPLOCI under the heading of Total comprehensive income attributable to: NCI

Other aspects of a group forex consolidation

Impact of future changes in exchange rates on the CSFP

There will be 2 impacts from movements in exchange rates between SFP dates: firstly, the value of net assets will change and, secondly, profits will be retranslated at different rates (average and closing rate)

The cost of investment is restated each year in the consolidation to allow for movement in exchange rates. This means that goodwill is restated at the year-end as it is deemed to be an asset of the subsidiary and therefore restated just like any asset

Changes will be taken to OCI in the CSPLOCI and so the NCI will take its share of any adjustment

Translation of a foreign currency loan

The **opening amount** should be translated at the rate applicable on the **last day** of the previous accounting period or the **first day** of the current accounting period

Interest for the year carried to the **income statement** should be translated at the **average** rate for the year

Interest paid in **cash** should be translated at the rate applicable on the **date** of that payment (spot rate) – in an exam scenario, this is likely to be the **closing rate**

The balance carried forward at the year-end should be translated at the **closing rate**

As a result of using the various different rates within the above, there will always be an **exchange gain or loss** to consider as a balancing item – make sure you consider carefully whether you are dealing with a liability or an asset to decide if the movement is a gain or loss

Intragroup loan outstanding (net investment in a foreign operation)

The following rules apply to monetary items which are part of the net investment in a foreign operation on consolidation:

> If the monetary item is denominated in the functional currency of the **parent** entity, the exchange difference will be recognised in the profit or loss of the foreign **subsidiary**

> If the monetary item is denominated in the functional currency of the **subsidiary**, exchange differences will be recognised in the profit or loss of the **parent** entity

> If the monetary item is denominated in the functional currency of **either** entity, then on consolidation the exchange difference will be **removed from the CSPL** and will be recognised **through OCI** and recorded in **equity** in the CSFP

> If the monetary item is denominated in a **third** currency which is different from either entity's functional currency, the translation difference should be recognised as part of the **profit or loss of the group**

> If the foreign operation is subsequently **disposed of**, the **cumulative** exchange differences previously reported as **OCI** and recognised in **equity** should be **reclassified** and therefore included in the **profit or loss on disposal** recognised in the **CSPL**

Groups – goodwill calculation

Suggested mark allocation in an FR question (CR Q2): 5-6 marks

Tip – mention the need for an impairment review!

As soon as you see that a goodwill calculation is required, get ready to mention at the **end** of your answer that an **impairment review** should be carried out on goodwill at **every year** end or earlier if there is an **indicator** of impairment.

Tip – mention the NCI!

Since you are performing a goodwill calculation, you are looking at a **group** scenario – therefore bear in mind our usual tip to always mention the **NCI** impact in group questions – if possible, try to calculate the **NCI at the year-end** i.e. the NCI amount used in the goodwill calculation as adjusted for the NCI share of events during the year (full **follow through** marking will apply here so please just try!)

Remember to comment on the **NCI share** of any adjustment in the goodwill calculation if NCI is measured as a **proportion of net assets** – the net assets will **change** as a result of the goodwill re-measurement so the **NCI share** of net assets will also change

Treatment

Always utilise the **FV** of consideration and the **FV** of assets and liabilities – this is the case even if the assets and liabilities would **not normally be carried at FV** in the financial statements

Important – do not forget to make the statement that **goodwill is not amortised** but is rather **tested annually for impairment** – then check the scenario: is there any indication of losses or changes in demand? These could be indicators of impairment

Acquisition-related transaction costs

These are **written off** to profit or loss – they are **not** included in the **consideration** figure

Contingent consideration

This should be measured at **fair value** in the goodwill calculation and a **corresponding liability** should be recognised (and then **unwound**) – remember to **categorise** the liability as **current** or **non-current** as appropriate

Discounting should be applied using the **company's cost of capital** – the discounted sum should be **added** to **consideration** when calculating goodwill

Make sure you refer to the **unwinding** of the **discount** on the liability, stating that this is taken to profit or loss as a **finance cost** and **increases** the **liability** – look out for **time apportionment** here – calculate the year end **liability** after the **unwinding** of the discount

Restructuring and future losses

The acquiring company should **not** recognise as **liabilities** any future **losses** or **other costs** expected to be incurred as a result of the business combination

A **plan** to restructure does **not** create a present obligation as a result of a past event (so it is not a provision) – additionally such a **plan** does not meet the definition of a **contingent liability** either

Recognition of intangible assets in the subsidiary

These may only be **recognised** separately from goodwill if they are **identifiable**

An intangible asset is **identifiable** only if it is **separable** (capable of being separated or divided and sold separately) or it arises from **contractual or other legal rights**

IFRS 3 gives some examples – these include customer lists and customer contracts

For customer lists to be separately recognised they must be **separable** or arise from **contractual or legal rights** – previously unrecognised internally-generated lists **might** be recognised on acquisition of a new subsidiary if they are deemed to be **separable** or arise from **contractual or legal rights**

IFRS 3 states that a customer list acquired in a business combination does **not** meet the criterion of **separability** if the **terms** of **confidentiality** or other **agreements prohibit** the entity from selling, leasing or otherwise exchanging information about its customers

Recognition of contingent liabilities

Normally, under IAS 37, contingent liabilities are not **recognised**, but only **disclosed** – in other words, no monetary value or related calculation regarding the contingent liability is applied within the financial statements and the users are simply given a **narrative explanation** that the contingent liability may exist

In the case of a **business combination**, however, contingent liabilities of the acquired company **are recognised** if the fair value can be measured reliably (it is **not** necessary for the outflow to be **probable**)

After initial recognition as part of the business combination process, the contingent liability should be recognised at the **higher** of the amount that would be recognised under IAS 37 and the amount initially recognised

Adjustments after the initial calculation of goodwill is complete

If **provisional** values have been used, the acquiring entity should retrospectively recognise any **adjustments** to those provisional values if the adjustments become apparent **within 12 months of the acquisition date** i.e. **replacing** the provisional figures with the new figures for the purposes of the goodwill calculation (adjusting the **carrying amount** of assets and **goodwill** as necessary)

Any further adjustment **outside the 12 month** period should only be recognised to correct an **error** rather than an estimate.

If further information in relation to an **estimate** emerges **after** the expiry of the 12 month period, this is **not** taken into account – only **errors** should be so adjusted

Remember to comment on the **NCI share** of any adjustment in the goodwill calculation if NCI is measured as a **proportion of net assets** – the net assets will **change** as a result of the goodwill re-measurement so the NCI share of net assets will also change

Deferred consideration – equity shares

Apply the **FV** of the shares on the date the consideration is recognised (usually the acquisition date)

Deferred consideration – cash

Apply the **FV** of future cash receivable – this is the same as the present value of the cash receivable

Apply a **discount rate** for the relevant number of years before the cash is payable – remember to **start** this from the **date the consideration is recognised/the acquisition date** and **not** from the **end** of the accounting period (unless (unusually) the acquisition occurs on the final day of the accounting period)

As with all discounting, remember to mention that the **unwinding** of the discount will be a finance cost in profit or loss – look out for **time apportionment** here – add this amount to the value of the initial asset to state the **year end carrying amount** of the asset

Deferred tax on goodwill – consolidated goodwill versus purchased goodwill

Tax authorities look at individual financial statements and charge tax on individual entities – they do not recognise goodwill that arises on consolidation as this relates to an asset of a group and the tax authorities do not tax groups as such (only the individual entities within the group)

IAS 12 indicates that **no deferred tax is recognised on goodwill** arising in a business combination (but this does not mean there are no deferred tax implications of a business combination – see our **Deferred tax** notes starting on page 38)

Note that the tax authorities may recognise purchased goodwill i.e. where an individual company purchases the assets and liabilities of a target rather than shares – the assets and liabilities are measured at FV and compared to the consideration – the entity may therefore have "purchased goodwill" rather than creating goodwill on consolidation

If the treatment of the "purchased goodwill" is **different** in the **financial statements** compared to the **tax treatment**, then deferred tax could arise

Fair value adjustments

IFRS 3 requires all assets and liabilities to be re-measured at **fair value** – this will override the carrying amount used in the accounts

Remember that for consolidation purposes you should depreciate the assets based on this **higher** fair value – try to state the **additional** depreciation that this will cause, and look out for **time apportionment** – remember to mention that this will **reduce profits** for the year

(In exam papers, it is much more likely that FV will exceed the carrying amount but in an exceptional circumstance where the FV is lower, the group depreciation charge would be lower.)

Groups – impairment and NCI

Suggested mark allocation in an FR question (CR Q2): 5 marks

If the NCI is based on the **fair value** or "full goodwill" method, there is no complication here

> Allocate an impairment loss against both the parent's goodwill and the NCI figure

If the NCI is based on the **proportion of net assets** method, it is necessary to apply a "**notional goodwill**" approach as explained in this section

This is because under the proportion of net assets the NCI is valued purely on the basis of net assets whereas goodwill is, by definition, a **difference** over and above consideration paid as compared to net assets i.e. it is an **additional** amount over and above net assets

Notional goodwill adjustment – calculation of the figure

Leave the parent's calculated goodwill figure as it is – no adjustment here

The notional NCI goodwill is calculated by **grossing up** the above parent figure and taking the NCI share of this

For example, if the NCI is 20% then apply a fraction of 20/80 or if the NCI is 30% then apply a fraction of 30/70, and so on

The result of this calculation will then "**absorb**" some of the total impairment loss, rather than this being taken by the parent – see below

Notional goodwill adjustment – allocation of the impairment loss

After calculating the above notional goodwill figure for the NCI, add it to the NCI value and then allocate the impairment loss based on the parent's goodwill figures and the adjusted (increased) NCI figure (as with the NCI at FV method)

However, the portion allocated to the NCI is only **notional** so it is **not recognised** in the consolidated P&L (only the parent's share is) – make sure you clearly explain this and provide relevant figures

See also page 110 of these Exam Room Notes

Groups – step acquisition

Suggested mark allocation in an FR question (CR Q2): 6 marks

Here the parent acquires control over the subsidiary in **stages**, by buying **blocks** of shares at different times

Full IFRS 3 acquisition accounting should only be applied when **control** has been achieved – until control is achieved any pre-existing interest is accounted for in accordance with IAS 39 for **investments** and IAS 28 for **associates and joint ventures**

If the 50% boundary is crossed, the entity should **revalue** its holding and report any **gain or loss** in profit or loss for the year – if the 50% boundary is not crossed, no gain or loss is reported and instead there is an adjustment to the parent's **equity**

There are 3 potential scenarios

> **Investment** to subsidiary (e.g. 10% holding to 60% holding)
>
> **Associate** to subsidiary (e.g. 35% holding to 60% holding)
>
> Increase in a holding which was **already** a controlling holding (e.g. 55% to 60% holding)

Scenarios 1 and 2 – Investment or Associate becomes a subsidiary

Consideration paid to acquire control (at fair value)	X
NCI (either at fair value or the proportion of net assets method)	X
Fair value of previously held equity interest at acquisition date	X
Less fair value of net assets of acquiree	(X)
= Goodwill	

In other words, compare what you are **now paying** and the value of what you **currently hold** against the value of all the net assets of the acquired entity, net of the NCI.

Reclassification adjustments on achieving control

If the previously held equity was classified as an **AFS** financial asset, any gains which were previously recognised in OCI should be **reclassified** from OCI to profit or loss

If the previously held equity was classified as an **investment in an equity accounted associate** and a share in the associate's **revaluation surplus** was recognised, this surplus should now be **transferred within reserves** from the **revaluation surplus** to **retained earnings**

Scenario 3 – Acquisitions that do not result in a change of control

No gain or loss is recognised

Goodwill is not re-measured

The difference between the fair value of consideration paid and the change in the NCI is recognised directly in **equity attributable** to owners of the parent

For example, if the entity **already** has **control** of a subsidiary and purchases a **further 10%** shareholding for £200,000 resulting in the NCI decreasing by £150,000 (as the NCI no longer holds the 10% sold) then a balancing amount of £50,000 would be debited from the parent's equity

Debit	NCI	150,000
Debit	Shareholders' equity	50,000 (balancing figure)
Credit	Cash	200,000

Groups – step disposal

Suggested mark allocation in an FR question (CR Q2): 6 marks

There are 3 potential scenarios

> Subsidiary to **Associate** (e.g. 70% holding to 30% holding)
>
> Subsidiary to **Investment** (e.g. 70% holding to 15% holding)
>
> Subsidiary to subsidiary (e.g. 70% holding to 60% holding)

As in the case of step acquisitions, the first 2 scenarios can apply the same pro forma approach

Scenarios 1 and 2 – subsidiary to Associate and subsidiary to Investment

Here there is a loss of control so a gain or loss on disposal is calculated using the following formula

Proceeds	X
Fair value of interest retained	X
less net assets of subsidiary prior to disposal (Working)	(X)
= Profit/Loss	X/(X)

Working	
Net assets	X
Goodwill at disposal	X
less NCI	(X)
= net assets of subsidiary prior to disposal	X

For a subsidiary to Associate disposal

Equity account as normal by reference to the year-end holding – the carrying value of the associate is based on the fair value of the interest as included within the gain calculation pro forma above

Consolidate results up to the date of disposal based on the pre-disposal holding

Equity account for results after the date of disposal based on the post disposal holding

Include the gain or loss on disposal as calculated in the pro forma

Amounts recognised in OCI in relation to the subsidiary should be accounted for in the same way as if the parent company had directly disposed of the relevant assets i.e. recycle amounts into OCI for AFS assets or transfer a revaluation surplus to group retained earnings for revalued assets

For a subsidiary to Investment disposal

The interest retained is initially recorded at fair value as included within the gain calculation pro forma above

Consolidate results up to the date of disposal based on the pre-disposal holding

Include dividend income after the date of disposal

Include the gain or loss on disposal as calculated above

Amounts recognised in OCI in relation to the subsidiary should be accounted for in the same way as if the parent company had directly disposed of the relevant assets i.e. recycle amounts into OCI for AFS assets or transfer a revaluation surplus to group retained earnings for revalued assets

Scenario 3 – subsidiary to subsidiary

Here there is no loss of control – therefore no gain or loss on disposal is calculated and no adjustment is made to the carrying value of goodwill. The difference between the proceeds received and the change in the NCI is accounted for in shareholder's equity i.e. as a balancing credit to shareholder's equity:

Debit	Proceeds (cash or receivables)	70,000
Credit	NCI	30,000
Credit	Shareholders' equity	40,000 (balancing figure)

Part disposal from an Associate holding (Associate to Investment)

For example, there may be a change from 40% holding to a 10% holding

Here there is a loss of significant influence so a gain or loss on disposal is calculated using the following formula

Proceeds	X
Fair value of interest retained	X
less Working (see below)	(X)
Profit/Loss	X/(X)

Working	
Cost of investment	X
Share of post-acquisition profits retained by Associate at disposal	X
Impairment of investment to date	(X)

The interest retained is initially recorded at **fair value**, as included within the gain calculation

Equity account for results up to the date of disposal based on the pre-disposal holding

Include dividends received after the date of disposal as dividend income

Include gain or loss on disposal as calculated above

Groups – subsidiary

Suggested mark allocation in an FR question (CR Q2): 6-8 marks for consideration of control and the goodwill calculation

Treatment

Is "control" achieved?

Under IFRS 10, an acquisition should be treated as a subsidiary and therefore consolidated if ownership indicates "control" of the entity

Ownership of more than 50% of share capital is a strong indicator that the owner has more than half of the voting power and therefore has "control"

Assessing control under IFRS 10 – advanced points

Note – only include these points if the matter of control appears complicated in the scenario – in most group answers, you would not need the below details

IFRS 10 states that an investor controls and investee if and only if it has all the following

> power over the investee

> exposure, or rights, to variable returns from its involvement with the investee

> the ability to use its power over the investee to affect the amount of the investor's returns

The fact that board members may not have actually exercised control in practice is not a determining factor in deciding whether the entity has control over the investee

We also need to consider powers to appoint board members – if there are such appointment powers for board members other than the entity which has a majority shareholding, then the matter may not be so straightforward and the shareholding greater than 50% may not be sufficient to create "control"

In some cases, control of board decisions over a fundamental aspect of the company such as R&D or finance e.g. if the owner can appoint a specific Director to be the head of R&D or Finance could also confer control if that division is fundamental to the investee

The right to acquire further shares through a call option could also be relevant – IFRS 10 requires an investor to consider potential voting rights in considering whether it has control and whether they are substantive i.e. whether the holder has the practical ability to exercise the right

If "control" is not held, the investment cannot be recognised as a subsidiary and would be recognised instead as an associate

Goodwill calculation

See page 89 of these Exam Room Notes.

Remember that **IFRS 3** requires all assets and liabilities to be stated at **fair value** – look out for additional asset value and contingent liabilities which will affect the net assets position

Contingent liabilities are not **recognised** in the individual statements but per IFRS 3 such liabilities must be **recognised** at **fair value** in the goodwill calculation

Groups – subsidiary to associate

Suggested mark allocation in an FR question (CR Q2): 4 marks

Remember to **time apportion** the events – treat as a **subsidiary** for the months during the year until disposal takes place – this would mean **consolidating** in the relevant number of months to the CSPL and recording an NCI at the relevant percentage at the end of the same period

After disposal, check whether there is still an **ability to influence** the disposed of subsidiary e.g. the ability to appoint directors to the board

If so, state that the entity should be treated as an **associate** and the **equity accounting method** should be used for the remaining X months of the year (the months **following** the sale)

> State that in future years the entity will make a **lower contribution to group profit** due to the **reduction** in the **percentage** investment held

State that a gain or loss on disposal occurs and calculate this if possible – use the following pro forma

Proceeds	X
FV of interest retained	X
NCI at disposal	X
less net assets at disposal	(X)
less remaining goodwill at disposal	(X)
Gain or loss on disposal	X

Check for any **dividends** – if these are declared whilst the entity is **still a subsidiary** then they should be **eliminated** on consolidation but if the dividend is physically paid **after** the disposal (and thus after the change to an associate) then remember **not to deduct** the amount from the net assets at disposal (as the **cash** is still held)

Groups – subsidiary to subsidiary

Suggested mark allocation in an FR question (CR Q2): 4 marks

Example: an entity holds 80% of a subsidiary and sells 20% of the subsidiary

Treatment

The subsidiary **remains** a subsidiary – under IFRS 3 there is **no disposal** but rather a transaction between group shareholders – there is no crossing of an accounting boundary which will result in any change in control so **no gain or loss** will be recorded – a **fair value** exercise is **not** required

The parent is treated as **selling a stake** (e.g. 20%) **to the NCI**

The NCI is **increased** in the SFP to reflect its greater share of the subsidiary

The difference between the consideration received from the NCI and the increase in the NCI (i.e. the value of the additional share now owned by the NCI) is taken as an adjustment to the parent's equity by crediting or debiting the group retained earnings

Consideration received	X
Increase in NCI on disposal	(X)
Adjustment to parent's equity (through group retained earnings)	X

The matter does not affect the **trading** profit of the company and so has no impact on the **P&L** or **EPS**

Hedge accounting – cash flow hedge

Suggested mark allocation in an FR question (CR Q2): 4 marks

General process

State why the hedge is being treated as a **cash flow** hedge – the entity is hedging a **variability** in cash flows for currency or other reasons (e.g. interest rate changes on a loan)

> A **firm commitment** is a binding agreement for the exchange of a **specified quantity** of resources at a specified price on a specified future date or dates – a **foreign currency** firm commitment can be subject to **either** a **cash flow** hedge or a **fair value** hedge

> A hedge of a **forecast transaction** (an uncommitted but anticipated future transaction) **must** be a **cash flow hedge** – the forecast transaction should be **specifically identifiable** (i.e. not something such as "the last 5,000 units produced"), **highly probable** and with a **party external** to the entity – the documentation should identify the **date** on which, or time period in which, the forecast transaction is **expected to occur** (the exact date is not required, but a reasonably specific and narrow range of dates should be stated)

Recognise entries at **inception** of the hedge – note that **often** the **derivative** will have **zero fair value** on this day and there may be no related cash transaction to record so there will be no figure to recognise for the derivative at inception – however, if the derivative is an option, for example, then **cash** may have been spent on the **premium** and this **cost should be capitalised** into the asset as an initially recognised amount

Even if no amounts are recognised at inception, the existence of the contract and associated risk should be **disclosed** from the **inception** date in accordance with IFRS 7

Any **transaction costs** such as professional fees should be **expensed**

Update entries at the year-end – the derivative will have gained or lost fair value with an **opposite** entry to the **P&L** for the underlying the hedged item

> Perform an effectiveness test to determine if the FV **movement** of the **derivative** is within 80-125% of the FV **movement** in the underlying item

For a **cash flow hedge**, the effective portion (i.e. the movement in the derivative **up to** the movement in the hedged item) is **recorded in OCI and held in a cash flow reserve** until the transaction takes place – any other portion ("ineffective") is put through the P&L

The amount stored is **released** into the P&L over the same period that the underlying item has its effect on the P&L e.g. as depreciation or interest expense/income hits the P&L

Treatment

Recognise the cost of the derivative itself on the SFP (but **expense** any transaction costs such as professional fees)

Dr Derivative asset

Cr Cash/Payables

Review the hedge for **effectiveness** i.e. derivative must move by 80-125% of the movement in the underlying hedged item – remember that it is possible to designate **only part** of the underlying item as being hedged e.g. if the item has a value of $5m but a derivative which hedges only $4.5m has been entered into then it is possible (**at inception**) to designate only $4.5m of the underlying value as being hedged – this will **improve hedge effectiveness**

Update the derivative asset/liability for the **fair value at the end of the year** – the **effective** portion is taken through **OCI** and the **ineffective** portion must be recognised in the **P&L** (the whole amount should be recognised in the **P&L** if the hedge falls **outside** the 80-125% effectiveness range)

Recycle any amounts of stored up in OCI into the P&L over the same period that the **underlying item affects the P&L**

Treatment – fixed price option

If the hedged contract is a fixed price option (i.e. an option to purchase a machine for $5m) then the fair value at inception is $5m translated into sterling at the spot rate – this is because we can determine what it would be reasonable to pay in sterling for the right to buy at $5m

This will give the derivative an initial fair value at **inception** – the fair value at the **reporting date** will then be $5m divided by the closing rate

Please note that this is a different treatment to a **currency option** which will normally have a **nil** value at inception as exchange rates will not have moved on the inception day so there is no FV to recognise

Possible purchase of a machine

If the question wording refers to a "**highly probable**" transaction then this is a reference to an "forecast transaction" and **must** therefore imply that you need to look at a **cash flow** hedge (since a fair value hedge can only be applied to an "firm commitment")

Remember **not** to **recognise** the machine in the financial statements until the **risks and rewards** of ownership have been transferred to the entity (this does not happen simply because a transaction is highly probable i.e. just because hedge accounting can be applied does not mean that the underlying item is recognised in the financial statements) – it is quite common for an exam question to try to trick you into **capitalising** equipment simply because there is a highly probable forecast transaction (the client accountant may already have made this mistake)

Summary of conditions for hedge accounting

At inception of the hedge, there is a **formal designation and documentation** of the hedging relationship and the entity's **risk management objective** and **strategy** for undertaking the hedge

The hedge is expected to be **highly effective**

The **effectiveness** of the hedge can be reliably assessed

The hedge is **assessed for effectiveness** on an **ongoing basis**

In respect of a **cash flow hedge**, a forecast transaction is **highly probable**

Hedge accounting – fair value hedge

Suggested mark allocation in an FR question (CR Q2): 4 marks

General process

State **why** the hedge is being treated as a **fair value** hedge – the entity is concerned that the underlying item could have a less favourable fair value at the time the transaction takes place

A **firm commitment** (the item being hedged) is not **recognised** – however the existence of the contract and associated risk would be **disclosed** from the inception date in accordance with IFRS 7

Recognise entries at **inception** of the hedge – note that **often** the **derivative** will have **zero fair value** on this day and there may be no related cash transaction to record so there will be no figure to recognise for the derivative at inception – however, if the derivative is an option, for example, then **cash** may have been spent on the **premium** and this **cost should be capitalised** into the asset as an initially recognised amount

Even if no amounts are recognised at inception, the existence of the contract and associated risk should be **disclosed** from the **inception** date in accordance with IFRS 7

Any **transaction costs** such as professional fees should be **expensed**

Update entries at the year-end – the derivative will have gained or lost fair value with an **opposite** entry to the **P&L** for the underlying hedged item

> Perform an effectiveness test to determine if the FV **movement** of the **derivative** is within 80-125% of the FV **movement** in the underlying item

> A **firm commitment account** may be needed to recognise an asset or liability (depending on exchange rate movement) as the opposite side of the derivative transaction

For a fair value hedge, the accounting is relatively straightforward as **both** movements in the value of the hedged item and hedging instruments go into the P&L

Foreign currency firm commitment

A hedge of a **foreign currency firm commitment** may be accounted for as a FV hedge **or** as a cash flow hedge at the **choice of the entity**

> A firm commitment is a binding agreement for the exchange of a specified quantity of resources at a specified price on a specified future date or dates

> A hedge of a forecast transaction (an uncommitted but anticipated future transaction) must be a cash flow hedge

If the hedged risk is identified as the forward exchange rate, rather than the spot rate, then it could be assumed to be perfectly effective if a forward is taken out as the hedging instrument

Final entries in a FV hedge – example of hedge over the purchase of inventories

On settlement, the inventory is purchased at the agreed rate, translated at the spot rate on the day of purchase

The value of the **firm commitment** then needs to be removed from the SFP, **adjusting the initial carrying amount of the inventory** as the other side of the double entry – this should set the effective purchase price (spot rate on the date of purchase, adjusted for hedging gain or loss) to that involved in the **initial** exchange rate when the hedge was set up

For example, if the **FV of the inventory has increased** since the hedge was set up, a firm commitment **liability** will have built up over time – this is then debited to close the account down at settlement and the credit side goes against inventory to reduce the cost of that purchase down to what it would have been at the time the hedge was set up (i.e. fixing it to that initial amount)

When using **FV hedging**, do not forget to **adjust** the **initial carrying amount** of the hedged item for this aspect to ensure that the entity has not gained nor lost out as a result of changes over time

Summary of conditions for hedge accounting

At inception of the hedge, there is a **formal designation and documentation** of the hedging relationship and the entity's **risk management objective** and **strategy** for undertaking the hedge

The hedge is expected to be **highly effective**

The **effectiveness** of the hedge can be reliably assessed

The hedge is **assessed for effectiveness** on an **ongoing basis**

Hedge accounting – general

The reason to apply hedge accounting is to ensure that the changes in value in the hedged item and changes in value in the hedging instrument are reflected in the financial statements in the **same period**

Derivatives are always measured at **FVtPL** but the underlying hedged item **may not be** – applying hedge accounting creates an accounting alignment

IAS 39 requires the hedge to be **designated** and **documented** at inception – documentation cannot be **backdated** and hedge accounting cannot be applied **retrospectively**

The **effectiveness** of the hedge must be tested **at least every reporting date**

Hedge documentation – points which should be included

Hedge type and hedged risk

Hedged item

Hedging instrument

Method of assessing hedge effectiveness

Derivative instruments

Transaction cost versus instrument cost

Be careful – **transaction costs** such as professional fees should **not** be treated as resulting in an **initial cost** for the item but if the item has a **cost to purchase** (e.g. the premium on an option) then this amount **should** be treated as part of the **initial cost** of the item and **capitalised** – therefore changes in fair value at the year-end should take into account this initial cost (i.e. deduct the cost from the year-end FV to find the movement to take to the P&L)

Therefore if the question only mentions **transaction costs** then the item will have a **nil value** at inception – if the question mentions **other types of cost** then the item will **not** have a **nil value** at inception

Example – a purchased option costs £50,000 and has a fair value of £1m at the year-end – the initial cost recognised is £50,000 and the movement in fair value is £950,000 for the year (not £1m)

Splitting intrinsic value from time value on an option

The change in fair value of an option is a mixture of a change in the **intrinsic value** (the gain or loss if exercised today) and **time value** (value from the amount of time remaining to expiry during which time the option may become more or less valuable)

The entity can **designate** the change in the **intrinsic value only** as the hedging instrument rather than the **total change** in fair value of the instrument – this could affect whether the hedge is **effective** or not

Remember that the designation must be made at **inception** and **cannot be amended retrospectively** simply to meet the hedge effectiveness criterion

Hedge accounting – hedge of a net investment

Suggested mark allocation in an FR question (CR Q2): 4 marks

This type of hedge only applies to a **group** scenario – the parent company takes out a **liability** in a foreign currency to create an opposite movement which hedges its **asset** i.e. a subsidiary which uses that same foreign currency

If the subsidiary **loses** value due to a change in the exchange rate, the company will experience a **counterbalancing gain** on its liability, and vice versa

This type of hedge is treated like a **cash flow hedge** i.e. the **ineffective** portion should be recognised in the **P&L** with the **effective** portion being recognised in **OCI**

Hedge documentation

The usual hedge documentation is required for this hedge i.e.

> **formal documentation** at **inception** of the hedge
>
> **identification** of the **hedging instrument** i.e. the loan
>
> **identification** of the **hedged item** i.e. the net investment in the subsidiary
>
> **details** of how hedge **effectiveness** is to be calculated
>
> a statement on the entity's **risk management objective** and **strategy** for undertaking the hedge

Treatment

The usual effectiveness criterion of **80%-125%** must be met in the case of this type of hedge

You should compare the **loss/gain** on translation of the net investment with the exchange **loss/gain** on the hedging loan

The portion of the gain/loss on the loan which relates to the parent's translation gain/loss in the **translation reserve** should be recognised in OCI and therefore directly in equity – the balance affects the **NCI**

The **ineffective** portion should be recognised in the **P&L** for the year – therefore if the loan moves by **more** than the change in the parent's translation reserve then the **excess amount** goes to the P&L and **not** through **OCI**

Hedge accounting – IFRS 9

Note – the 2018 Corporate Reporting Study Manual has added text to indicate that the impact of IFRS 9 on future accounting periods is now **more examinable** than in prior years

Please use the following notes **with caution** as we do **not** expect a **huge number** of marks to be available for this issue

Problems with IAS 39 hedge accounting rules

Considered to be **complex** and not reflective of the way in which an entity normally **manages** its risks

Often **prevents entities applying hedge accounting** to transactions which have **genuinely** been entered into for hedging purposes and which do involve a **hedging effect in practice**

IFRS 9 – impact on the entity and auditors

IFRS 9 is effective for reporting periods commencing on or after **1 January 2018**

Adoption of IFRS 9 rules on hedge accounting will require the **entity** to have appropriate processes in place to identify **new hedging opportunities** and to ensure that the extensive new disclosure requirements of IFRS 9 are met

Auditors will need to test management's judgements with regard to the hedge effectiveness criteria (the "**economic relationship**" test – see below) and will also need to obtain comfort over the fair value measurement of the components of non-financial hedged items, purchased options, forward contracts and cross currency swaps

IFRS 9 approach – basics

Applies a **principles-based** approach (compared to the **rules-based** approach of IAS 39)

Use of a principles-based approach will require **judgement** in relation to the determination of whether a hedging relationship meets the **hedge effectiveness criteria** (the "**economic relationship**" test – see below) and the determination of when "rebalancing" will be required (see below)

Aims at **better alignment** with the risk management practices actually used by **management**, allowing transactions which are **genuinely intended to be hedges** to **apply hedge accounting** in situations where **IAS 39 rules may preclude this**

Allows **both** derivatives and non-derivative financial assets or liabilities to be hedging instruments, provided that they are measured at Fair Value through Profit or Loss – IAS 39 requires hedging instruments to be **derivatives** except for the hedge of foreign currency

Replaces the **IAS 39 "bright line" 80% - 125% test** with an "**objective-based assessment**", designed to create an assessment more closely aligned with the actual practices of companies in managing their risks

Requires an "**economic relationship**" between the hedged item and hedging instrument – in other words, the hedging instrument and the hedged item must have values that generally move in opposite directions because of the same risk (which is the hedged risk)

Allows **changes to the hedging relationship** if the risk management objective for that designated hedging relationship remains the same – this is known as "**rebalancing**" – IAS 39 generally requires discontinuation of hedge accounting if there is a change in the hedging relationship

IFRS 9 approach – discontinuation of hedge accounting

Voluntary discontinuation of hedge accounting is **not permitted** when the risk management objective for the hedging relationship has not changed

This is a notable **contrast** with IAS 39 rules which allow an entity to **revoke hedge accounting at any time**

As such, **discontinuation** of hedge accounting is a **rare instance** where the **IFRS 9** rules are **less flexible** than the **IAS 39** rules

IFRS 9 and IAS 39 – shared rules

The following 4 points have not changed under the IFRS 9 approach

> the **terminology** of the standards is generally the same

> the **3 types** of hedge (fair value hedge, cash flow hedge and hedge of a net investment) are the same

> hedge **ineffectiveness** is recognised in **profit or loss** (except for the Other Comprehensive Income option for equity investments, which is a category only available under IFRS 9)

> hedge accounting with **written options is prohibited**

IFRS 9 approach – more complex points

Allows the **time value** of purchased options and the **forward element** of forward contracts and foreign currency basis spreads to be **excluded** from the hedging relationship, which should decrease volatility in profit or loss – under IFRS 9 the time component of an option is a cost of hedging presented through **OCI** (rather than in the P&L) and the forward element of forward contracts may also be presented in **OCI** (rather than in the P&L)

Allows **more items** to be designated as **hedged items** than under IAS 39 – examples include risk components of non-financial items, groups of items and net positions even if the change in value attributable to the hedged risk is not proportional to that of the designated items within the group (unlike under IAS 39) and equity investments at Fair Value through Other Comprehensive Income (this category does not exist under IAS 39)

May be beneficial to **banks** – under IAS 39, banks do not often achieve hedge accounting on the **credit risk of exposures** due to certain complications with the rules – IFRS 9 will make it easier to achieve hedge accounting on this type of risk

Does **not permit** hedge accounting to apply when **credit risk dominates the value changes** that result from an otherwise qualifying "economic relationship"

Holiday pay accrual

Suggested mark allocation in an FR question (CR Q2): 2 marks

Treatment

IAS 19 requires an accrual to be made for **holiday entitlement carried forward** to the next year

Calculate (1) the number of days carried forward **on average per employee**

Calculate (2) entity's **total number of working days in a year** e.g. number of employees multiplied by (purely as an example) 48 weeks x 5 days per week or 240 days (check the question wording to determine the number of working days in the year for the entity)

The accrual should then be based on the **number of days carried forward** (1) divided by the **total number of working days in the entity's working year** (2) multiplied by **total annual salary costs**

In other words you are finding the share of total annual salary costs which relates to the proportion of days carried forward to the next year as holiday

The journal is likely to be

Dr   Employee expenses (P&L)

Cr   Accruals (SFP)

Impairment

Suggested mark allocation in an FR question (CR Q2): 4-8 marks

Assets should not be carried at more than their **recoverable amount** which is the **higher** of **value in use** and **FV less CTS**

> Value in use is the **present value** of the **future cash flows** expected to be derived from an asset (**excluding** finance and tax costs)

Impairment is recognised **immediately** in profit or loss unless the asset has **previously been revalued**, in which case it is treated as a **revaluation decrease** and not as an impairment loss (it is first set against the revaluation surplus on the same asset, with any excess being recognised in profit or loss)

Indicators of impairment

Only **material** impairment needs to be identified – if there are indicators of **possible** impairment, the entity is required to make a formal estimate of the recoverable amount of the assets concerned

External indicators

A **fall** in the asset's market value that is more significant than would **normally** be **expected** from the passage of time through normal use

A significant **change** in the technological, market, legal or economic **environment** of the business in which the assets are employed

An **increase** in market interest rates or market rates of return on investments likely to affect the **discount rate** used in calculating **value in use**

Carrying amount of the entity's net assets being more than its **market capitalisation**

Internal indicators

Evidence of **obsolescence** or **physical damage**

Adverse changes in the **use** to which the asset is put

Indications that the **economic performance** of an asset is, or will be, **worse than expected**

Always perform annual impairment tests on the following 2 items

> An intangible asset with an **indefinite** useful life

> **Goodwill** acquired in a business combination

Asset with a revaluation surplus

First recognise the **impairment** against the revaluation surplus

If there is still a further amount to recognise **after the revaluation surplus** has been reduced to **nil** then the **remainder** of the impairment charge should be recognised as part of **profit or loss**

Impairment – CGU

Suggested mark allocation in an FR question (CR Q2): 6 marks

Anticipated **future losses** indicate that equipment/a CGU could be **impaired**

The impairment review involves comparing the **carrying amount** of the equipment in the financial statements with the **recoverable amount** – if the recoverable amount is **lower** than the carrying amount, the difference should be **written off** in the **P&L** for the year and **deducted** from the **carrying amount** in the **SFP**

Recoverable amount is defined as the **higher** of

> FV less CTS
>
> value in use

FV less CTS is the price that would be received in an **orderly** transaction between market participants at the measurement date, net of any selling costs

Value in use is the present value of expected future cash flows from the CGU, discounted at a rate the market would expect for any equally risky investments

Normally the cash flow should be estimated over a **maximum of 5 years** – if a period above this figure is used this should be **disclosed** (the **validity** of the disclosed explanation should be **reviewed** as part of the audit)

Allocation of impairment losses – order of allocation

First allocate as much as possible against **goodwill**

Then allocate against **other assets** on a **pro-rata** basis, based on **carrying value**

> However, **no asset** should be reduced below the **higher** of its **recoverable value** and **zero**
>
>> Therefore assets such as **cash**, **inventories** or **receivables** should **not** take any impairment as these should already be at recoverable value

Treatment of NCI interest in goodwill of a CGU – proportion of net assets method of valuing NCI

Notionally adjust the NCI share in goodwill by grossing it up **temporarily** for impairment purposes only – add this **notional** amount onto the goodwill balance available to be reduced for impairment (i.e. the first target in the allocation of the impairment loss as this is **first allocated** against goodwill and then **pro rata** against other assets)

However, the **actual impairment loss** recognised is the parent's share only – the **notional amount** is only used to determine how the total impairment loss is used up

The consequent impairment loss calculated is only recognised to the extent of the parent's share

Example

An NCI of 40% is valued on the net assets method – goodwill held by the parent is therefore 60% of the total goodwill for notional purposes – therefore NCI share is **40 / 60** x goodwill held by the parent

If the parent's goodwill is 90 then we would add on 40 / 60 x 90 or **60 of notional goodwill** to provide up to **150 of goodwill** against which to allocate impairment but only take the parent's (60%) share of that allocated impairment into account when reducing goodwill and charging the P&L

For example, here we would take only **60%** of the impairment allocated to goodwill when reducing the parent's figure of **90** down to the relevant amount

Under the FV method of valuing NCI no such special adjustment is required before allocating impairment

Reversal of a CGU impairment

Goodwill impairment is not **reversed** once recognised

Impairment of **other assets can** be reversed pro-rata to the carrying amount of those assets

The revised carrying amount may not, however, be increased above the **lower** of

> **Recoverable amount**, and

> **Depreciated carrying amount** assuming that no impairment loss had originally been recognised

The reversal is recognised in the **P&L** except where reversing a loss recognised on assets carried at revalued amounts which are treated in accordance with the applicable IFRS

Insurance Contracts

IFRS 4 was issued in **2004** as an **interim** solution which **permits** the **continued use of pre-existing national reporting frameworks** whilst seeking to prevent **certain undesirable practices** – the standard also aims to **reduce divergence** amongst the practices used in different countries

IFRS 4 specifies the financial reporting for **insurance contracts** by an entity that issues such contracts or holds reinsurance contracts – it only relates to these contracts and **not** to the **assets** and **liabilities** held by insurers **generally**

IFRS 4 focuses largely on improving **disclosure requirements** but contains a number of limited improvements to existing **accounting** requirements – these are **best practice** examples and not requirements if other practices are currently adopted

The contract must relate to an **uncertain event** i.e. an event with **uncertainty** with respect to **at least one** of the following: **occurrence, timing** or the **level of compensation** to be paid by the insurer

The contract must have significant **insurance risk** (**non-financial** risk relating to whether an event occurs, rather than a change in a financial variable) or IFRS 4 will not apply

Examples of insurance contracts

Life insurance and prepaid funeral plans

Disability and medical cover

Credit insurance

Travel cover

Examples which are not insurance contracts

Product warranties

Defined benefit pensions

Licences or contractual rights/obligations contingent on the use of a non-financial item

A finance lease with a residual value guarantee

Financial guarantees within the scope of IAS 39

Contingent consideration that has arisen as a result of a business combination

Insurance contracts that the entity holds as policyholder

Recognition and measurement

IFRS 4 **exempts** an insurer temporarily from the **usual need to consider the IASB Framework where there is no specific accounting requirement** set out in another international standard – this exemption is **temporary** whilst further rules on insurance contracts are being developed by the IASB

However IFRS 4

      Requires a **liability adequacy test** to be performed

Prohibits **provisions** for possible claims under contracts that are **not in existence** at the reporting date (**catastrophe** or **equalisation** provisions)

Requires an **impairment test** for reinsurance assets – impairment is recognised if an event has occurred that will lead to amounts due under the contract not being recovered in full and a reliable estimate of the shortfall can be assessed

Requires an insurer to continue to **recognise** insurance liabilities until they are discharged, cancelled or expire – offsetting liabilities against related reinsurance assets is not permitted

Liability adequacy test

Recognise insurance liabilities based on the current estimate of future contractual cash flows – recognise any identified shortfall **immediately** as part of the profit or loss for the period i.e. the amount carried in the accounts may not be sufficient compared to this calculated amount

Should be based on **all** contractual cash flows and related costs such as claims handling costs – cash flows relating to embedded options or guarantees should also be included – deduct any deferred acquisition costs and related intangible assets

If the accounting policies of the insurer do not demand a liability adequacy test then the amount that should be recognised under IAS 37 should instead be used, **increasing** the **liability** recognised if necessary

Disclosures

The insurer must disclose

Information which "**identifies and explains amounts arising from insurance contracts**" – accounting policies adopted, identification of recognised assets, liabilities, income and expense arising from insurance contracts

Risk management objectives and policies of an entity should be disclosed to explain how an insurer deals with the **uncertainty** it is exposed to

An entity is not generally required to comply with the disclosure requirements of IFRS 4 regarding comparative information that relates to annual periods beginning before **1 January 2005** but comparative disclosure is required in relation to accounting policies adopted and the identification of recognised assets, liabilities, income and expense arising from insurance contracts

Future accounting periods – IFRS 17

In May 2017, **IFRS 17** Insurance Contracts was issued by the IASB

IFRS 17 introduces a comprehensive reporting framework for insurance contracts that is intended to result in insurance companies producing financial statements which are **more comparable, consistent** and **transparent**

Implementation of IFRS 17 will cause **significant challenges** for **entities** and **auditors** – there will be changes to **profit recognition patterns**, increased **volatility of profit and equity** and **increased options** and **requirements for judgement** to be exercised – **disclosures** should become more **transparent**

Please refer to pages **605** and **606** of the 2018 CR Study Manual if further detail is required

Intangibles

Suggested mark allocation in an FR question (CR Q2): 4 marks

Definition

An **identifiable** non-monetary asset without physical substance

Must be **separable** or **arise** from contractual or legal rights to be **recognised**

Treatment

There must be **probable** future economic **benefits** that are **attributable to the asset** which will flow to the entity and it must be possible to measure **cost reliably**

Initial recognition should be **at cost**, including **directly attributable** acquisition costs

> Exclusions **not** treated as **directly attributable costs**: costs of **introducing** a new product or service including costs of **advertising** and **promotional** activities, costs of **conducting** business in a new location or with a **new class** of customer (including staff **training**) and **administration** and other **general overhead** costs

Amortisation should be charged and recognised in the P&L – look out for **time apportionment** here

State the **year-end** carrying amount after amortisation

Subsequent expenditure is **not** normally recognised

Expenditure to be treated as an expense (i.e. **not** capitalised)

Start-up costs

Training costs

Advertising and promotional costs

Business relocation and reorganisation costs

All **research phase** expenditure such as search costs, design costs and so on

> Activities aimed at obtaining new knowledge

> Search for, evaluation and final selection of applications of research findings or other knowledge

> Search for alternatives for materials, devices, products, processes, systems or services

> Formulation, design, evaluation and final selection of possible alternatives for new or improved materials, devices, products, processes, systems or services

Capitalisation of development costs

To be capitalised, **all** the following criteria must be met

> **Technical** feasibility

Intention to use or sell the asset

Ability to **use or sell** the asset

Asset will generate probable future economic **benefit**

Availability of adequate **technical, financial** and **other resources** to complete the development and to use or sell the intangible asset

Ability to **measure reliably** the expenditure attributable to the intangible asset during its development

Examples of expenditure which would qualify for capitalisation

Design, construction and testing of pre-production or pre-use prototypes and models

Design of tools, jigs, moulds and dies involving new technology

Design, construction and operation of a pilot plant that is not of a scale economically feasible for commercial production

Design, construction and testing of a chosen alternative for new or improved materials, devices, products, processes, systems or services

Specific internally generated intangible assets which cannot be recognised

Internally generated brands, mastheads, publishing titles and customer lists

The reason is that these costs **cannot be identified separately** from the cost of **developing** the **business as a whole**

Intangible assets acquired as part of a business combination

IFRS 3 provides 5 examples of types of intangible which **should** be recognised separately from goodwill

Marketing-related intangible assets such as **trademarks**

Customer-related intangible assets such as **customer lists**

Artistic-related intangible assets such as **motion picture films**

Contract-based intangible assets such as **franchise agreements**

Technology-based intangible assets such as **computer software**

Intangible assets acquired as part of a **business combination** are normally considered to meet the recognition criteria of IAS 38 – the assets should be measured at FV

Amortisation of an intangible

The amortisation charge should reflect the **pattern** in which the asset's future economic benefits are consumed – if such a pattern cannot be predicted reliability, the **straight-line method** should be used

Residual value should be assumed to be **zero unless** a third party is committed to buying the intangible asset **at the end of its useful life** or unless there is an **active market** for that type of asset and it is probable that there will be a market for the asset at the end of its useful life

The amortisation period and method used for an intangible with a **finite** useful life should be reviewed at each year end

Revaluation of an intangible

Revaluation may be allowed if it can be shown that an **active market** exists for the asset – a revaluation model similar to IAS 16 can then be used (i.e. include the revaluation in a Revaluation surplus in the SFP)

Note that an **offer** from another party to buy the asset **could** suggest that an **active market** exists – however, the items traded must be **homogeneous (absolutely identical)**: in most cases, the items will be **different** in **some** way

> Items such as copyrights, publishing rights and film rights have unique sale values so are **not** homogeneous (**no active** market)

> Items such as fishing rights or quotas or taxi cab licences are **identical** so could qualify for revaluation treatment (**active** market)

Interim Financial Reporting

Not mandatory

IAS 34 does **not** make interim financial reporting **mandatory** – however, interim financial reporting is **strongly encouraged**

IAS 34 encourages **publicly-traded** entities to provide an interim financial report for at least the **first 6 months** of their financial year and to make this report available **no later than 60 days** after the **end** of the interim period

The report can either be a **complete** set of financial statements at the interim date complying **in full with IFRSs** or a **condensed** interim financial report prepared in compliance with **IAS 34's** special requirements

Minimum components

Condensed SFP

Condensed SPL and OCI (either as a single statement or as 2 separate statements)

Condensed SoCIE

Condensed SCF

Selected note disclosures

Periods covered

SFP	End of the current interim period and comparative data at the end of the most recent financial year
SPL and OCI	For the current interim period and cumulative data for the current year to date, together with comparative data for the corresponding interim period and cumulative figures for the previous financial year
SCF	Cumulative to the current year to date with comparative cumulative data for the corresponding interim period in the previous financial year
SoCIE	Current interim period and for the year to date, together with comparative data for the corresponding interim period and cumulative figures for the previous financial year

Materiality

Should be assessed in relation to the interim period financial data – should be recognised that interim measurements rely to a greater extent on estimates than annual financial data

Recognition and measurement principles

In general, the same recognition and measurement principles should be used in its interim statements as it does in its annual financial statements (e.g. on assets and accruals)

Revenue items received occasionally, seasonally or cyclically

Should **not** be **anticipated** or **deferred** (accruals or prepayments) in interim financial statements **if** it would be **inappropriate** to anticipate or defer the revenue in the **annual** financial statements

Costs incurred unevenly during the financial year

Again, follow the same principles as in the full annual financial statements

Appropriate to **anticipate** a cost for property rental where the rental is **paid in arrears**

Inappropriate to **anticipate** part of the cost of a major advertising campaign later in the year, for which no expenses have **yet been incurred**

Payroll taxes or insurance contributions paid by employers

In some countries, these amounts are paid **unevenly** during the year, with most amounts paid **earlier** in the year and a small part in the **second half** of the year – in this case, an estimated average annual tax rate for the year can be used rather than the **actual** cash tax paid

This treatment is appropriate because the taxes are assessed on an annual basis

Cost of a planned major periodic maintenance or overhaul

A **planned event** later in the year must **not** be **anticipated** unless there is a **legal** or **constructive obligation** to carry out this work

The fact that such work is carried out **annually** is **not of itself** sufficient to justify **anticipating** the cost

Other planned but irregularly occurring costs

Should **not** be accrued in an interim report – even if they occur regularly and are planned, they are **discretionary**

Year-end bonus

Should **not be provided** for unless there is a **constructive obligation** to pay a year-end bonus (e.g. a contractual obligation or a regular past practice) and the size of the bonus can be reliably measured

Holiday pay

If there is an enforceable obligation on the employer then any **unpaid** accumulated holiday pay may be accrued in the interim financial report

Non-monetary intangible assets

Follow the normal principles of IAS 38 – IAS 34 does **not allow** the deferral of cost in the expectation that it will eventually be part of a **non-monetary intangible asset** that has not yet been recognised – such costs should be treated as an **expense** in the interim statement

Depreciation

Should only be charged in an interim statement on non-current assets that have been **acquired, not** on non-current assets that **will be acquired** later in the year

Forex gains and losses

Apply the usual principles of IAS 21 with respect to the rates to be used

Tax on income

Apply the estimated **average** annual tax rate for the year based on the **best estimate** of expected profits for the year – this is **appropriate** because **tax** is charged on an **annual** basis and not on interim figures

Therefore also take into account anticipated tax credits based on annual figures

Losses should **not** be anticipated – charge tax based on the profits made in the period and then if the losses do subsequently happen later then record a **negative tax charge** for that later period as required

Inventories

Apply the **normal IAS 2 principles** – but it is recognised that it will be necessary to rely more heavily on **estimates** for interim reporting than for year-end reporting

NRV should normally be estimated from **selling prices** and **related costs** to complete and dispose of at interim dates

Inventories

Suggested mark allocation in an FR question (CR Q2): 3 marks

Inventories should be held at the **lower** of **cost** and **Net Realisable Value (NRV)**

> If it is necessary to **write down** the value of inventories then this amount should be recognised in the **P&L**

> NRV must be assessed at the **end of each period** and compared with **cost** – this could result in the **reversal** of all or part of the original write-down

Cost includes the **costs of purchase**, **conversion** and **other costs** involved in bringing the inventories to their present location and condition

> **Fixed production overheads can** be **included** in cost but on the basis of the **normal** capacity of production facilities (taking account of capacity lost through **planned** maintenance)

> **Variable production overheads** should be based on the **actual** use of production facilities

> Therefore low production or idle plant will not result in a higher fixed overhead allocation to each unit

> **Unallocated** overheads must be recognised as an **expense** in the period in which they were incurred

> If production is **abnormally high** the fixed production overhead allocated to each unit will be reduced, so avoiding inventories being stated at more than cost

Costs which would not be included in the cost of inventories

Abnormal amounts of wasted materials, labour or other production costs

Storage costs other than costs that are necessary in the production process before a further production stage

Administrative overheads not incurred to bring inventories to their present location and condition

Selling costs

Cost formulae

Only the **FIFO** and **weighted average cost methods** are allowed under IAS 2 – LIFO is not aLlowed.

Cost methods

Standard costs – set up to take account of normal levels of raw materials used, labour time etc – these are reviewed and revised on a regular basis

Retail method – often used in the retail industry where there is a large turnover of inventory items with similar profit margins

Non-application of IAS 2

IAS 2 does not apply to

> **work in progress** under **construction contracts**
>
> **financial instruments**
>
> **biological assets**

Investment Property

Suggested mark allocation in an FR question (CR Q2): 4 marks

Treatment

IAS 40 permits 2 **alternative** accounting treatments: the **cost and depreciation model** as under IAS 16 or the **fair value** model specific to IAS 40 – whichever policy is chosen by the entity, it must be applied to **all** of its investment property

> Even if the **cost model** is adopted, the FV of investment property must be **disclosed**

Under the **fair value** model any change in the value of the property is recognised in the **P&L**

An entity that chooses the **FV model** should measure **all** of its investment property at **FV** (unless, exceptionally, this cannot be measured reliably, in which case IAS 16 should be used)

Criteria

The property must be held to earn **rental** or **capital appreciation** or **both**, rather than being **used** in the **ordinary course of the business** (i.e. not owner-occupied, unless the owner-occupation is **insignificant** in certain situations – see below)

Recognise the property as an investment property when it is **probable** that the future economic benefits that are associated with the investment property will **flow to the entity** and the **cost** of the investment property can be measured **reliably**

Transaction costs

Recognise only those costs which are **directly attributable** to the investment property such as **professional fees** and **property transfer taxes**

Self-constructed investment property

Property being **self-constructed** or under development for **future use** as an investment property qualifies as an **investment property**

Leases

If held under a **lease** and **classified as an investment property** then it shall be accounted for as if it were a **finance lease**

Entity occupies part of property and leases out the balance

If the 2 portions can be **sold separately or leased separately under a finance lease** then each is accounted for separately as appropriate i.e. one part could be an investment property and the other part(s) could be PPE, or vice versa

If the portions **cannot** be **sold** or **let** separately then the **entire property** can be treated as an investment property if only an **insignificant** portion is **owner-occupied**

Entity supplies services to the lessee of the property

The property is only an investment property if the services are **insignificant** to the **arrangement as a whole**

Property leased to and occupied by a parent, subsidiary or other group company

The property can be an **investment property** in the entity's own accounts but would be **owner-occupied** (not an investment property) from a group perspective

Changes in use

Example	Accounting treatment
Commencement of owner occupation	Start to apply IAS 16 – if FV model was in use when an investment property then treat FV as the deemed cost on transfer
Commencement of development with a view to sale	Reclassify as inventory under IAS 2 – if FV model was in use when an investment property then treat FV as deemed cost
Development with a view to continued letting	Continue to treat as investment property
End of owner occupation with a view to letting out	Start to apply IAS 40 – if FV model will be used under IAS 40 then revalue at the date of change and recognise the difference as a revaluation under IAS 16
Property held as inventory now let out	Start to apply IAS 40 – if FV model will be used under IAS 40 then revalue at the date of change and recognise the difference in profit or loss
Commencement of operating lease to another party	Start to apply IAS 40

Change in use from PPE to investment property

Account for the property under **IAS 16** up to the date of change in use

If the **revaluation model** is used, account for any **difference** between its carrying amount and its fair value at this date in accordance with IAS 16 i.e. recognise a gain in OCI and as a revaluation surplus

Depreciation should **cease** at the date of change in use

From the date of change in use, IAS 40 applies – the entity may apply IAS 40 on either a fair value basis or in line with IAS 16 – always check the entity's specific policy here

If the property is held at **fair value** under IAS 40, any **year end gain** should be debited to the asset account and credited to the P&L for the year

Remember **not to depreciate** the property once it qualifies as an IAS 40 investment property

Fair value

The fair value should reflect **market conditions** at the reporting date – a valuation which reflects **special circumstances** or a buyer who is **not knowledgeable** of local market conditions should not be used

Professional fees

IAS 40 **permits** the inclusion of **certain costs** within the **capitalised** amount of an investment property

Professional fees and installation of new **capital equipment** are likely to be acceptable but inclusion of **relocation costs** would **not** be – relocation costs should be **expensed** in the P&L

Building does not qualify as investment property under IAS 40 – IAS 16 probably applies

If the IAS 40 criteria are failed, remember to briefly state the IAS 16 criteria instead

Remember that the revaluation model can be used under IAS 16 – a revaluation gain is **stored up** in the **revaluation reserve** and recognised in **OCI until sale** rather than hitting the P&L

Depreciation should be charged, reducing the carrying value

Entity occupies the building

The building cannot be an investment property if the entity **occupies** and **uses** a "**significant part**" of the building and the vacant part is not capable of being leased or sold separately – in this case the **whole building** should be treated as a normal owner-occupier building

If the lessor provides services as part of the rental agreement and those services are **more than "insignificant"**, then classification as an investment property is **not** permitted – for example, the lessor could provide basic services such as maintenance and security whilst correctly treating the property as an investment property but if the lessor were to provide **administrative support** or **training services** to the tenant then these would **not** be "insignificant" and the activity would not be investment but rather a form of trading so the property should be treated as owner-occupied

If the entity uses only a **very small proportion** and the rest of the building cannot be sold or leased separately it is acceptable under IAS 40 to treat the **whole building** as investment property

Property is being developed for future sale

Such a building cannot qualify as an investment property – the building must be treated in accordance with IAS 2 until such time as it is **ready for disposal**

Initial recognition should be at **cost** but it should be written down to NRV if this falls below cost

Establishing fair value

IAS 40 states that fair value must be measured in accordance with IFRS 13 which defines fair value as "the price that would be received to sell an asset in an orderly transaction between market participants at the measurement date"

IFRS 13 requires entities to **maximise** the use of **observable** inputs and **minimise** the use of **unobservable** inputs

Level 1 – **quoted** prices in **active markets** for **identical** assets or liabilities

Level 2 – **observable prices other than quoted prices** e.g. quoted prices for **similar** assets **in active markets** or prices for **identical assets in non-active markets**

Level 3 – **unobservable inputs** i.e. models using the entity's own assumptions about market value

In the case of investment properties, a Level 2 input as possible if there are similar buildings being sold in an active market

Downturn in market value

If this has genuinely arisen **after** the year-end, it will be a non-adjusting event after the reporting period and the change in market value should be **disclosed** (rather than **recognised**) in a note to the accounts

If it is possible to measure the value reliably, this value should be used

Audit point

It is generally recommended that the entity should use an **external expert** in property valuation but IAS 40 does **not require** this

Disclosure points

The entity should disclose

> whether the entity has followed the FV model or cost model

> whether property interests held as operating leases are included in investment property

> criteria for classification as investment property

> assumptions in determining FV

> whether there has been use of an independent professional valuer (encouraged but not required)

> rental income and expenses

> any restrictions or obligations

> if applying the FV model – a reconciliation of the carrying amount of the investment property at the start and end of the period

> if applying the cost model – depreciation method, rates and useful lives as well as a reconciliation of the carrying amount at the beginning and end of the period – in addition, an entity which adopts the cost model **must disclose the FV** of the investment property even though the FV amount is not used/recognised within the financial statement figures themselves

Joint Arrangements

Suggested mark allocation in an FR question (CR Q2): 4 marks

Joint operation

An arrangement **not structured** through a separate entity is **always** a joint operation – the parties that have joint control (the joint operators) have rights to the assets and obligations for the liabilities of that joint arrangement

An arrangement structured through a separate entity **could be either** a **joint operation** or a **joint venture**, depending on the rights and obligations of the parties to the arrangement

Each party to the joint operation recognises its **share** of the assets, liabilities, revenue and expenses of the joint operation

Joint venture

Joint control of an entity is split between different parties – **usually** there will be a **separate entity** set up

There is a **contractual arrangement** to share profits and losses and the parties have rights to the net assets of the arrangement

Apply the **equity method** – recognise the investment at cost and then add the **share of the joint venture's post-acquisition change in net assets** (**generally** the change in net assets will be caused by the **profits and losses** of the investment) – look out for time apportionment here

The **share** of the joint venture's post-acquisition change in net assets will be recognised in the **P&L**

The investment will be shown as a **non-current asset** in the SFP

An investor in a joint venture is a party to the joint venture but which does not have **joint control** over the joint venture – if there is **significant influence** then an Associate exists: if there is no **significant influence** then the accounting should be as a financial asset

Transactions between a venturer and a joint venture

If a venturer sells an asset to the joint venture at a profit and the asset is still held by the joint venture then

> the proportion of the asset that is consolidated **includes an element of profit recorded by the venture**

> this amount should be **removed** as it is **unrealised profit**

> the remainder will be only the profit that relates to the share of the assets relating to the **other** venturers

If a venturer **purchases** assets **from** the joint venture the venturer's **share of the profit** made by the joint venture should **not** be recognised until the asset is sold to a third party

If a **loss** is made on a transaction between the venture and joint venture then it should be recognised **immediately** if it represents a **reduction** in **realisable value** of current assets or an **impairment loss**

Receivables and payables with the joint venture should **not** be eliminated

Leases – dealer/manufacturer

Suggested mark allocation in an FR question (CR Q2): 6 marks

Treatment

This treatment applies if the dealer/manufacturer makes a sale under a **finance lease**

Recognise a **receivable** equal to the **net investment** in the lease

The seller recognises separately (1) its **normal selling profit** and (2) its **finance income from the lease**, based on **discounting** and then **unwinding** that discount on the cash flows under the lease

Calculate initial **sales revenue** as the **lower** of the **fair value of the asset** and the **present value** of the **minimum lease payments**, computed at a market interest rate

Calculate **cost of sales** as the **lower** of **cost of production** and **carrying amount less PV of the unguaranteed residual value** – apply this to the initial sales revenue to find the **profit** to be recognised **now**

Calculate **finance income** from the lease – start with the sales revenue figure identified above and deduct any **initial payment made** – then unwind the discount at the applicable interest rate and update the year end net investment in the lease

Split the net investment between receivables falling due within **one year** and receivables falling due **after more than one year** – remember to go **one column to the right of next year's payment** in your lease payment schedule to obtain the amount falling due **after** more than one year – the amount falling due within one year is then a **balancing** amount

Example (amounts in the lease liability table are not exact but purely illustrative)

A dealer sells an item under a finance lease. The FV is £26,250 and the PV of the MLP is £23,000. Purchase price of the item is £21,000.

Revenue to recognise now is £23,000 and profit to recognise now is £23,000 - £21,000 or £2,000. We also need to recognise some finance income on the finance lease so set up a table with £23,000 (revenue) as the initial figure and then the final year end figure in the table is a receivable to be recognised in the SFP (this can be further split into current and non-current portions if you have time by extending the table by a further year and then looking 1 column to the right of next year's payment)

	b/f	Payment	Capital	Interest	c/f
This year	23,000	(9,000)	14,000	5,000	19,000
Next year	19,000	(9,000)	10,000	4,000	14,000

Receivable of 19,000 can be split into 10,000 non-current (look at next year's row and then one column to the right of next year's payment) and 9,000 current as a balancing item (again these figures are purely for **illustration**)

Do not forget to mention the **finance income** (P&L) and the **receivable** (SFP) as well as the revenue/profit aspects (P&L) – make sure you state the year-end receivable as updated for finance income and cash received

Leases – finance leases

Suggested mark allocation in an FR question (CR Q2): 6 marks

The IAS 17 factors which would normally indicate that a **lease** is a **finance lease** are as follows

the lease **transfers** ownership of the assets at the end of the lease term

the lessee has the **option to purchase** the assets at a price sufficiently below fair value at the option exercise date and it is **reasonably certain** the option will be exercised

the lease term is for the **major part** of the asset's economic life even if title is not transferred

the present value of the MLP amounts to **substantially all** of the assets fair value at inception

the lessee is responsible for the **insurance** and **maintenance** of the asset

the leased asset is **so specialised** that it could only be used by the lessee without major modifications being made

cancellation losses are borne by the lessee

fluctuations in fair value at the **end** of the lease accrue to the lessee

the lessee has an **option to extend** the lease for a secondary period at a **peppercorn rent** i.e. below market rent

Treatment – lessee's financial statements

Recognise any assets at the **lower** of PV of MLP and fair value

Recognise a corresponding **liability**

Charge a **finance cost** based on the **interest rate implicit** in the lease and recognise this in **finance costs** in profit or loss – look out for **time apportionment**

If the lease is paid **in arrears**, calculate the **interest** based on the **opening figure** for the year

If the lease is paid **in advance**, deduct the cash payments from the **opening figure** for the year **before** calculating interest

Charge **depreciation** based on the initially recognised amount – look out for **time apportionment**

Show the **split** between current and non-current liability (see below)

Cancel out any **rental charges** if the client has **mistakenly** treated the item as an **operating lease** – there is no rental charge for a finance lease as the lessee is treated as purchasing the item outright over time

If it appears to be **relevant** (use your judgement to determine how many marks there are for the lease as compared to other matters) consider the **cash flow impact** of the lease – **physical cash** payments of **interest** should be recorded in the **SCF** and **repayment** of the **capital element** should be shown as part of "financing activities"

Example finance lease liability tables

Rentals in arrears

	b/f	Interest at 10%	Payment	c/f
2001 – CY	24,869	2,487	(10,000)	17,356
2002	17,356	1,736	(10,000)	9,092

Total lease liability at end of 2001 is 17,356

Non-current (one column to the right of next year's payment) is 9,092

Therefore the balancing current liability must be 17,356 - 9,092 or 8,264 (i.e. next year's payment net of next year's interest)

Rentals in advance

	b/f	Payment	Capital	Interest at 10%	c/f
2001 – CY	34,869	(10,000)	24,869	2,487	27,356
2002	27,356	(10,000)	17,356	1,736	19,092

Total lease liability at end of 2001 is 27,356

Non-current (one column to the right of next year's payment) is 17,356

Therefore balancing current liability must be 27,356 - 17,356 or 10,000 (i.e. next year's payment)

Finding the non-current liability

Remember the rule – always look **one column to the right of next year's payment** to find the non-current liability

> Therefore for a lease paid **in arrears** the current liability is equal to the cash payment **net** of next year's interest

> Therefore for a lease paid **in advance** the current liability is equal to the cash payment

Deposits

If an upfront **deposit** is required, deduct this from the **opening liability**

Land and buildings

Originally IAS 17 stated that a lease of land should be treated as an **operating lease** unless title is expected to pass at the end of the lease term

IAS 17 has now been **amended** so in the case of a **long lease** the risks and rewards do pass **regardless of the transfer of title** – therefore a lease of land **can** be a finance lease if it meets the existing criteria

Note that in the FAR Study Manual and FAR past paper model answers a lease of **40** years is considered a **long lease** and the related lease of land was treated as a **finance lease**

Leases – IFRS 16

Note: IFRS 16 will replace IAS 17 with effect from 1 January 2019 – **IAS 17 remains** the **main** standard examinable in Corporate Reporting so only ever include **brief** remarks on IFRS 16 (and only if you have time) – an additional section on IFRS 16 was added to the 2017 Corporate Reporting Study Manual and the 2018 Corporate Reporting Study Manual indicates that IFRS 16 may be examined within the context of how the financial statements may be affected in future years

IFRS 16 adopts a single model for all types of lease but **retains** the IAS 17 classification of a lease as a finance lease or an operating lease for **lessors** – for **lessees**, there is **no requirement to distinguish** between operating and finance leases

A **lease** is defined as a contract, or part of the contract, that conveys the **right to use an asset** (an "**underlying asset**") for a period of time in exchange for consideration.

> A lease does **not** arise if the **lessor** can **substitute** the underlying asset for another asset during the lease term and the **lessor** would **benefit economically from doing so** (for example, the lessor might benefit from the **convenience** of being able to select which particular asset (e.g. which particular machine) to provide to the lessee)

An **underlying asse**t is defined as an asset that is the subject of a lease, for which the right to use that asset has been provided by a lessor to a lessee.

The "**right to control**" the use the of asset requires the right to **obtain substantially all of the economic benefits from use** of the identified asset, and the **right to direct the use** of the identified asset

In cases where the contract includes a **lease element** and **also** an **element which is not a lease** (such as a service contract), the element which is not a lease must be **separated out** from the lease and **accounted for separately**.

Where a lease exists, a lessee will recognise a "right of use asset" initially measured at cost (plus lease payments made before the commencement date, less lease incentives, plus initial direct costs incurred plus dismantling and restoration costs that a lessee is obliged to pay at the end of the lease term)

The asset is then measured at cost less depreciation and impairment unless the revaluation model is used or the item is an investment property and the lessee applies the fair value model

The asset is depreciated over the shorter of the useful life of the underlying asset and the lease term

An election to apply simplified accounting can be used for a lease with a term of 12 months or less or a lease for a low value asset

IFRS 15 (revenue) guidance will be applied to **sale and leaseback** transactions to determine if a sale has taken place

If a sale has taken place, a gain or loss is recognised based on the value of the rights transferred to the buyer

If no sale has taken place, there is no derecognition and proceeds are treated as a financial liability under IFRS 9

IFRS 16 – illustration of concept of substitution and economic benefit to the lessor

User Ltd has entered into an arrangement with Provider Ltd regarding the use of certain machinery which will be used to produce car engine parts. Provider Ltd has agreed to provide User Ltd with any one of a selection of 10 similar machines on a weekly basis and has also agreed that the relevant machine must be able to produce 5,000 car parts per day. Provider Ltd can provide User Ltd with any of its 10 similar machines as required at its absolute discretion.

A lease **does not arise** because there is **no identifiable asset** and Provider Ltd (**the lessor**) can **substitute** the machine as it wishes, deriving **economic benefits** from doing so in terms of **convenience**.

User Ltd should account for the rental payments as **a normal expense** in the P&L rather than applying IFRS 16.

IFRS 16 sale and leaseback numerical example – calculation of gain

On 1 July 2016, First Ltd bought a specialised printing machine for £1.2m. The carrying amount on 30 June 2017 was £1.0m.

On 1 July 2017, First Ltd sold the machine to Second Ltd for £1.48m, which was the fair value of the machine. First Ltd immediately leased the machine back for 5 years (the remainder of its useful life) at £320,000 per annum payable in arrears.

The present value of the annual lease payments is £1.4m and the transaction satisfies the IFRS 15 criteria to be recognised as a sale.

Step 1 – calculate the accounting profit on disposal: 1.48m - 1m = 480,000

Step 2 – apply fraction of (PV of leaseback payments / FV of asset): 1.4/1.48 x 480,000 = 454,054

Step 3 – deduct amount found in step 2 from the amount found in Step 1: 480,000 - 454,054 = 25,946

Treat the amount from Step 3 as the gain to recognise immediately.

Note – a shortcut can be applied – the gain to recognise can be calculated simply as 0.08/1.48 x 480,000 = 25,946 – in other words, place the difference between the FV of the asset and the PV of leaseback payments (0.08 in this example) over the FV of the asset and apply this to the accounting profit on disposal – this will be slightly quicker to calculate

Leases – lease incentives

Suggested mark allocation in an FR question (CR Q2): 3 marks

Examples

A **rent-free** period or **reduced rent** on an **introductory** basis

Treatment

Accounted for under **SIC 15 Operating Leases – Incentives**

Recognise the **aggregate benefit** of the incentives as a **reduction** of rental expense **over the lease term**, on a **straight-line** basis

The client accountant will probably have recognised the incentive **upfront** and will therefore have calculated the rental expense for the year on a **cash basis** – this is likely to **understate** the expense as correctly calculated on an accruals basis since the **first year** of expense will be **too low** as **all** of the incentive has been taken **immediately**

It is therefore likely that you will have to **increase the rental expense** and have a corresponding credit to a **payables** account to allow for the missing accrual of rental expense

Calculation

The easiest approach is to find the **total payable** under the lease **excluding** the incentive, find the **total value of the incentive** and deduct this from the **total payable** and then **spread the resulting net amount equally per month** (as there will likely be some **time-apportionment** to consider so having a **monthly** figure will be helpful)

The amount paid in cash is **unlikely** to match the **accounting amount** recognised under SIC 15 so look out for an **accrual** or **prepayment** here and **quantify** this

Example

An entity takes out a 5 year operating lease over a building at an annual cost of £1m per year – the entity agrees a rent-free period of 6 months

The entity should not therefore recognise all of the incentive in the period where this is given in cash terms – for example, in the above example the rent-free period of 6 months should **not** be recognised upfront or all in the first year of the lease but rather the saved costs should be spread equally over the 5 years of the lease

Leases – operating leases

Suggested mark allocation in an FR question (CR Q2): 5 marks

An **operating lease** is any lease that is **not** a **finance lease**

Therefore it is a lease which does **not** transfer **substantially all the risks and rewards** normally associated with **ownership** of an asset

Treatment

No complicated treatment is needed for an operating lease – unlike for a finance lease

Lease expenses should be charged on a **straight-line basis** (unless another systematic and rational basis is more representative of the time patterns of the user's benefit) even if **cash** is not paid on this basis

Therefore look out for an **accrual** or **prepayment** as the cash payments are highly unlikely to match the amounts due under accounting principles

See also our section on lease incentives on page 132.

Land and buildings

Originally IAS 17 stated that a lease of land should be treated as an **operating lease** unless title is expected to pass at the end of the lease term

IAS 17 has now been **amended** so in the case of a **long lease** the risks and rewards do pass **regardless of the transfer of title** – therefore a lease of land **can** be a finance lease if it meets the existing criteria

Note that in the FAR Study Manual and FAR past paper model answers a lease of **40** years is considered a **long lease** and the related lease of land was treated as a **finance lease**

Disclosures

Accounting policy for operating leases

Operating lease payments charged as an expense for the period

In respect of non-cancellable operating leases, a commitments noted analysed into amounts due within 1 year, within 2 to 5 years and after more than 5 years

> Note that this is not an analysis of liabilities as with a finance lease – it is simply a listing of commitments – there will also by definition be no disclosure of finance charges for operating leases as there are no finance charges applicable to such leases

A general description of **significant** leasing arrangements

Mineral Resources

IFRS 6 deals with expenditures on **exploration for** and **evaluation of** mineral resources but not with **expenditures** incurred **before** the **acquisition** of **legal rights to explore** and **expenditures** incurred **following** the **assessment of technical and commercial feasibility**

Entities may change their policies under IFRS 6 as long as the new information is closer to meeting IAS 8 criteria

IAS 38 applies to the **development** of mineral resources – IFRS 6 only applies to **exploration and evaluation of resources** so it should not be applied when the technical feasibility and commercial viability of extracting a mineral resource are demonstrable

Measurement at recognition

Measure at **cost**, applying expenditure recognition policy consistently

Initially recognised cost may include acquisition of rights to explore, exploratory drilling, sampling, studies and activities relating to commercial evaluation

Record as **tangible** or **intangible assets**, as appropriate

Measurement after recognition

Apply **either** the **cost model** or **revaluation model** under IAS 16

Changes may be made if the change makes the financial statements **more relevant** to users, applying IAS 8 criteria

Impairment

IAS 36 is modified such that impairment tests are required

> When technical and commercial viability of **extraction** is **demonstrable**, at which point **IFRS 6 is no longer relevant to the asset**

> When other facts indicate that the **carrying amount exceeds recoverable amounts** such as exploration rights have expired, there has been no success in finding commercially viable mineral resources and the entity has decided to discontinue exploratory activities within a specific area or estimates suggest that the carrying amounts of assets are unlikely to be recovered in full following successful development of the mineral resource

If it is required, impairment testing is undertaken in accordance with IAS 36

Presentation and disclosure

Disclosure involves the **description** of the **accounting policies applied** and the **amounts** relating to assets, liabilities, income and expense as well as operating and investing cash flows arising from exploration for and evaluation of mineral resources

Once benefits are demonstrable, **other standards supersede IFRS 6** and the assets are reclassified accordingly

Onerous Contracts

Suggested mark allocation in an FR question (CR Q2): 3 marks

A contract in which the **unavoidable costs** of meeting the obligation under the contract **exceed** the **economic benefits** expected to be received under it

Unavoidable costs are the **lower** of the **cost** of **fulfilling** the contract and any **penalties** arising from **failing to fulfil** it

This means that the entity must only provide for the **lower** net cost of exiting the contract – this is because a **rational** entity will pick the **lower** cost so that is the **maximum** cost that it could incur and hence it is the amount of the provision

> **Be careful here** – it is **tempting** to use the **higher** figure on the grounds of **prudence** but, as indicated, the entity will not choose that option so it is not a relevant figure

Treatment

The present obligation under the contract should be recognised and measured as a **provision in the SFP**

> A present obligation from a past event exists (a lease was signed)

> An outflow of economic benefit is probable (rentals or a penalty will be payable)

> The amount can be measured reliably (future rentals or the penalty, discounted if discounting would make a material difference to the figure)

The **corresponding amount** should be recognised in the **P&L**

Operating Segments

Suggested mark allocation in an FR question (CR Q2): 2-3 marks

Note – there will not be **many** marks for IFRS 8 issues (unless a detailed numerical working is needed) but the marks that are available can be **obtained very quickly indeed**

Tip – if the question refers to a plc which is undergoing some kind of change (acquisition, disposal, restructuring) then this is probably a hint that there will be a couple of marks for IFRS 8 issues

IFRS 8 – only applicable to publicly traded entities

Only entities whose equity or debt securities are **publicly traded** need to disclose segment information under IFRS 8

In **group** accounts, only **consolidated** segmental information needs to be shown

Operating segment definition

A **component** of an entity that engages in business activities from which it may **earn revenues and incur expenses** (including revenues and expenses relating to transactions with other components of the same entity) …

… whose operating results are **regularly reviewed by the entity's chief operating decision maker** to make decisions about **resources to be allocated** to the segment and assess its performance …

… for which **discrete financial information** is available

The term "**chief operating decision maker**" refers to a function rather than to a manager with a specific title so need not refer to a particular individual

Aggregation

Two or more segments may be aggregated if the segments have **similar economic characteristics** and the segments are similar in **all** the following respects

> Nature of **products or services**
>
> Nature of the **production process**
>
> Type or class of **customer** for their products or services
>
> **Methods** used to **distribute** their products or provide their services
>
> Nature of the **regulatory environment**

Threshold for reportability

Determination of **reportable segments** – segment is **reportable** if

It is an operating segment and any of the following size criteria are met:

Segment revenue is at least **10%** of total (internal and external) revenue, or

Segment profit or loss is at least **10%** of the profit of **all** segments in **profit** (or loss of **all** segments making a **loss,** if greater)*, or

Segment assets are at least **10%** of **total** assets

At least 75% of total external revenue must be reported – if this is not the case based on those segments identified based on the above rules then **additional** segments must be added even if these **do not themselves** meet the 10% thresholds

*For the purposes of this test, look at **all profitable** segments and find **10% of the total profit** – then look separately at **all segments making a loss** and find **10% of the total loss** – do not calculate 10% of any figure which deducts losses from profits

Disclosures – segment-level

Segment disclosures

Factors used to identify the entity's reportable segments

Types of products and services from which each reportable segment derives its revenues

Operating segment **profit or loss, segment assets, segment liabilities, certain income and expense items including a reconciliation**

Disclosures – entity-wide

External revenue by each product and service

Geographical information: external revenue and non-current assets by entity's country of domicile and all foreign countries

Information about **reliance on major customers** which represent **more than 10% of external revenue**

Pension schemes – narrative on different types

Suggested mark allocation in an FR question (CR Q2): 3 marks

Please note: you will not necessarily need the below points in every pensions question – however, sometimes you may be asked to explain the different types of scheme to the client and the notes below should then be used

Defined contribution scheme (employee makes a specified contribution)

Accounting is more straightforward

Risk not reflected in the figures in the SFP – no need to include a liability on the SFP

The employer)and possibly employees) pay regular contributions of a "defined" amount each year

These amounts are invested and the **size of pensions paid to former employees depends on how investments perform**

Employees bear the risk that investments may not perform well

Defined benefit scheme (employer is responsible for providing a specified pension)

Accounting is much more complicated – the **FV of plan assets** and **PV of plan liabilities** must be calculated and disclosed

The size of pension benefits which can be claimed after employment is determined or "defined" in advance

The employer and possibly employees pay contributions into the plan with the size of the contributions set at an amount **expected to earn enough investment returns to meet obligations** to pay post-employment benefits

The entity bears the risk that the funds may be insufficient as the employer will be required to make up the shortfall

If assets are larger than the liability for postemployment benefits, the employer may be allowed to take a "**contribution holiday**"

Therefore if the **employer bears risk** the scheme is very likely to be a "**defined benefit plan**"

Additionally, if the entity bears a risk/has a liability in the case that an employee leaves the company and transfers the pension to another fund, then again the scheme is very likely to be a "defined benefit plan"

Pension schemes – pro formas and disclosures

Suggested mark allocation in an FR question (CR Q2): 6 marks

Typical client error – cash contributions treated as P&L charge

It is very common for the client accountant to treat the **cash contributions** to the plan assets as the accounting entry for the **P&L charge** for the year – this is incorrect as it does not reflect an **accruals** approach

The correcting entry will typically be

Dr Pension plan assets (SFP)

Cr Employee expenses – pensions (P&L)

This will cancel the expense incorrectly recognised by the client on a cash amount (i.e. no net impact on the P&L) whilst moving that payment correctly into the plan assets on the SFP

The 2 pro formas

Note that these pro formas **should not be the whole of your answer** – you also need to write up how the figures calculated in the pro forma are presented in the financial statements i.e. whether they are in the **P&L**, **OCI** or **SFP**

We recommend that you write figures for both pro formas as **positive** figures even for the PV of the obligation – this will reduce confusions with negative numbers and will mean that the benefits paid out to employees claiming a pension will be a **negative** entry in **both** columns (and in most cases the only such negative entry that applies to **both** columns)

We have tried to include **as many possibilities as possible** in the examples below – note that your answer will not necessarily need to use **all** the relevant rows

Change in the FV of plan assets

Fair value of plan assets at [first day of the period]	X
Interest on plan assets (P&L)	X
Cash contributions paid in during the year* (SCF)	X
Benefits paid out during the year (SCF)	(X)
Gain or loss on the re-measurement (OCI)	X/(X)
Fair value of plan assets at [final day of the period]	X

* This figure is likely to have been treated as the P&L charge by the client accountant (see above)

Change in the PV of the obligation

Present value of obligation at [first day of the period]	X
Interest cost on obligation (P&L)	X
Current service cost (P&L)	X
Past service cost (P&L) [unusual – see below]	X
Loss or gain on settlement (P&L) [unusual – see below]	X/(X)
Benefits paid out during the year (SCF)	(X)
Gain or loss on the re-measurement (OCI)	X/(X)
Present value of obligation at [final day of the period]	X

Remember to state in your answer where items are recognised in the financial statements – we have included reminders in brackets in the pro-formas above but you will also need to mention this in your answer – consider using the tabular presentation which can be found on the next page

Actuarial gains or losses

These must be recognised in OCI in the year in which they arise

Some double entries

Retirement benefits paid out

Debit   PV of defined benefit obligation (SFP)

Credit   FV of plan assets (SFP)

Contributions paid into plan

Debit   FV of plan assets (SFP)

Credit   Cash (SFP)

Past service cost – increase in obligation

Debit   Past service cost (P&L)

Credit   PV of defined benefit obligation (SFP)

Past service cost – decrease in obligation

Debit   PV of defined benefit obligation (SFP)

Credit   Past service cost (P&L)

Gain on settlement

Debit   PV of defined benefit obligation (SFP)

Credit   Past service cost (P&L)

Loss on settlement

Debit   Past service cost (P&L)

Credit   PV of defined benefit obligation (SFP)

Discount rate

The discount rate adopted should be the market yield on **high-quality fixed rate corporate bonds** – if there is no "**deep**" market for such bonds, the yields on **comparable government bonds** should be used instead

Past service costs and settlements

These relate to a change in the PV of the defined benefit obligation because of an **amendment** (change in benefits offered by a plan), **curtailment** (reduction in the number of employees covered by the plan) or **settlement** (transaction to eliminate employment benefit obligations)

Past service costs are recognised at the **earlier** of (1) when the plan amendment or curtailment **occurs** and (2) when the entity **recognises** related **restructuring costs** or **termination benefits**

All gains and losses arising from past service costs or settlements must be recognised **immediately** in profit or loss

Full disclosure pro forma

Important: use your judgement here – how many marks are available for pensions as compared to other parts of the question? You **may not need** to present these full disclosures …

At the same time, it is important to note that simply producing the change in PV of the obligation and change in the FV of plan assets pro forma is not enough (see above) to fully answer the question – you need to indicate to the examiner exactly **how these numbers are disclosed in the financial statements**, either in your narrative write-up or by the presentation of the tables noted below

Amounts recognised in the statement of financial position

	Current year	Prior year
Present value of obligation	X	X
Fair value of plan assets	(X)	(X)
Net liability	X	X

Expense recognised in profit or loss for the year ended XXXX

Current service cost	X
Net interest on the net defined benefit obligation*	(X)
[Other P&L items from the question]	X
Net expense	X

* As the defined benefit obligation will almost certainly exceed the fair value of the plan assets we have assumed that there will be a net interest expense (rather than net income) in the P&L

Amount recognised in other comprehensive income for the year ended XXXX

Actuarial loss on obligation	(X)
Return on plan assets excluding amounts in net interest	X
Net re-measurement loss*	(X)

* As there is almost always an actuarial loss in the question we have assumed that there is a net re-measurement loss here

Performance review – tips

General tips

Watch your **timing** – CR past papers have **not** tended to award a **high number of marks** for performance review (in contrast to the Question Bank questions which sometimes allocate an **entire 30 marks to performance review**) – therefore **do not try to be too ambitious**: there will be many marks available in the question for other areas/topics

Start with a data table – not only does this look good, it ensures that you know what the **big picture** is **before** you start writing – you can always supplement the data table with a few further calculations in brackets mixed into the narrative if you need to

Use plenty of **headings**, ensuring that you are **spreading** your points well and doing everything asked in the question wording – ensure that you refer to at least some extent to each **requirement** of the question – **do not write too much on the Income Statement** just because this is the **first part** of the question

Focus on the **bigger movements** and the **movements which can be explained from the scenario** – the examiner does not care if inventory days have moved from 46.3 to 46.7, particularly if there is nothing in the Exhibit information to explain this

Apply some **professional scepticism**, especially if **forecasts** are involved – there will **always** be **more information that you would like to have**

Look out for the **context** of the scenario – does this give **management** an incentive to be **unrealistic**? e.g. if the information is prepared for a bank as part of restructuring or to apply for a loan might this give a reason for unrealistic predictions?

Consider **further information** that may be needed – look for ratios that you would **like to calculate** but cannot calculate based on the figures – look for **contingent liabilities** or indications that asset values may differ under a FV approach

Think about the **user** of the report – a bank will want to see a good stream of **earnings** and **good interest cover** to repay interest and loan capital, an investor will want to know **dividend yield** and recent **EPS** figures

Again, remember that the **past exam papers** have **not** given **as many marks** for the performance review as the **example questions in the Question Bank** which are dedicated solely to performance review – do not go **overboard** with your CR review (**particularly if you are also doing SBM** – there will almost certainly be more marks in SBM for performance review)

Make **scenario-specific** points – explain the figures based on the scenario and suggested causes – do not just write in a load of numbers and changes **with no explanation**

Create **scenario-specific indicators** – revenue per store or per employee or gross profit per car etc will always be more interesting for the reader than "**standard**" points such as **revenue increase** or **gross profit margin** – **try not to use solely indicators that could be used in any question**

Further information points – add a few areas where **further information** would be useful but try to avoid **generic** points – make points that are **specific to the scenario** – try not have **too many further information points or you will run out of time quickly**

Try to offer a brief **conclusion** section under an appropriate heading

Profitability

Consider ratios such as margins, return on equity, return on capital employed

Try to use **scenario-specific indicators** – gross profit per shop (etc) so that your answer is **not generic**

Liquidity

Consider using ratios such as the current ratio, quick ratio, receivables days, payables days, inventory days

Look out for any need to pro-rate the assessment e.g. if assessing the 6 monthly accounts then use 180 days not 365 days for the working capital days ratios

Cash generation

Consider explaining why there is a difference between accounting profit/loss and cash generation

Further information example – general

Further analysis of revenue

Figures adjusted for exceptionals to understand true like-for-like changes

Geographical or segmental data such as locations of new offices or openings

Non-current asset disclosure information to understand depreciation policies and to make comparisons with industry averages – analysis of capital expenditure

Information on dividend policy

Details of future plans and management initiatives

Information on employees and employee numbers

Further detail on key cost categories

Details of the tax charge

Details of potential diluting financial instruments that could affect DEPS

Further information example – contingent liability

Report from the investigation into the issue to understand the likelihood of having to pay out on the issue and any monetary sums that may have to be paid

Information on whether a write-down of any items is needed

Information on press reporting of the issue to understand reputational damage

Post year-end information to determine the potential future impact of the issue

Whether safeguards have been put in place to prevent the issue happening again

Details of relevant contracts

Performance review – ratios

Important notice: do not spend too long on the numbers – **choose only the most relevant ratios**

Always start by first using the scenario-specific indicators given in the question (e.g. the client's own internal performance metrics) and only move onto these more "generic" analysis points **after** the scenario-specific indicators have been thoroughly used.

Performance ratios

$$gross\ profit\ margin = \frac{gross\ profit}{revenue}\ x\ 100\%$$

Replace gross profit with **operating profit to get operating profit margin**. This allows you to see whether cost of sales (gross profit) or admin costs (net profit) are more significant as a constraint on returns

$$return\ on\ capital\ employed\ [ROCE] =$$

$$\frac{PBIT + associate's\ post\ tax\ earnings}{equity + net\ debt}$$

Net debt = interest-bearing debt (current and non-current) less cash and cash equivalents

Equity = exclude redeemable preference shares, in line with general treatment as a loan, not equity

$$return\ on\ equity\ [ROE] = \frac{profit\ before\ tax}{equity\ or\ net\ assets}\ x\ 100\%$$

Note that ROE is quicker to calculate than ROCE and with less chance of error

$$return\ on\ shareholders'\ funds\ [ROSF]$$

$$= \frac{profit\ attributable\ to\ owners\ of\ parent}{equity\ less\ NCI}$$

Profit attributable to owners of parent will usually be profit after tax

Note the difference: ROCE uses profit **before** tax; ROSF uses profit **after** tax

You can remember this by thinking of ROSF as measure of what the shareholders get i.e. after tax, whereas ROCE is more of a measure of the capacity of the business to generate a return, and tax is then a subsequent cost to be considered later

Exam tip ROSF is usually quicker and easier to calculate; you can then comment that ROSF only looks at equity as a source of resources

Liquidity ratios

$$current\ ratio = \frac{current\ assets}{current\ liabilities}$$

Usually expressed as a multiple e.g. 3:1 (equivalent to 6/2)

$$quick\ ratio = \frac{current\ assets\ less\ inventories}{current\ liabilities}$$

Basically, the current ratio adjusted for inventories as these cannot be turned into cash very **quickly**.

Long-term solvency ratios

$$gearing = \frac{net\ debt\ as\ per\ ROCE}{equity\ as\ per\ ROCE}\ x\ 100\%\ \text{or}\ gearing = \frac{net\ debt}{net\ debt + equity}\ x\ 100\%$$

$$interest\ cover = \frac{PBIT\ plus\ investment\ income}{interest\ payable}$$

Efficiency ratios

$$net\ asset\ turnover = \frac{revenue}{capital\ employed}$$

$$receivables\ period = \frac{trade\ receivables}{revenue}\ x\ 365\ days$$

$$payables\ period = \frac{trade\ payables}{cost\ of\ sales}\ x\ 365\ days$$

Strictly, use credit purchases but usually you will have to use cost of sales

Investor ratios

$$dividend\ cover = \frac{earnings\ per\ share}{dividend\ per\ share}$$

$$price\ earnings\ ratio = \frac{market\ price\ per\ share}{earnings\ per\ share}$$

Other ratios

$$CAPEX\ to\ depreciation = \frac{capital\ expenditure\ (CAPEX)}{depreciation}$$

Measures whether new expenditure compensates for depreciation.

$$non-current\ asset\ ageing = \frac{accumulated\ depreciation}{non-current\ assets\ at\ cost}$$

Allows an estimate of how far non-current assets are through their working lives e.g. if depreciation is £2m and the assets cost £4m, then we are 2/4 = 50% through its working life.

Note: the above two ratios require data on depreciation. Hence they are subject to the depreciation method/charge decided upon by management (i.e. subjective).

$$dividend\ yield = \frac{dividend\ per\ share}{current\ market\ price\ per\ share}\ x\ 100\%$$

Cash flow ratios

Least likely to be possible to calculate in CR but included for completeness

Note: the concept of "cash return" is important here and is used in several ratios

cash return = cash generated from ops + interest received + dividends received

$$cash\ ROCE = \frac{cash\ return}{capital\ employed\ as\ per\ ROCE} \times 100\%$$

$$cash\ from\ operations\ as\ \%\ of\ profit\ from\ operations = \frac{cash\ generated\ from\ operations}{profit\ from\ operations} \times 100\%$$

$$cash\ interest\ cover = \frac{cash\ return}{interest\ paid}$$

$$cash\ flow\ per\ share = \frac{cash\ return - interest\ paid - tax\ paid}{number\ of\ ordinary\ shares}$$

$$cash\ dividend\ cover = \frac{cash\ return - interest\ paid - tax\ paid}{equity\ dividends\ paid}$$

Only look at equity dividends.

The result of (cash return – interest paid – tax paid) is also known as "cash flow for ordinary shareholders".

Provisions

Suggested mark allocation in an FR question (CR Q2): 4 marks

Criteria for recognition

Present obligation as a result of a **past** event

Probable outflow of resources

Amount can be **reliably estimated**

Make sure you **apply these to the scenario** by using **examples** from the examination paper

Discounting

If the impact of time value would be **material**, then the provision should be **discounted** – if the provision amount relates to an **asset** (e.g. machinery) then it should be **added to the cost of that asset**, increasing the depreciation charge over the lifetime of the asset by (discounted amount / life of the asset)

Remember to mention **unwinding of the discount** which creates a **finance cost** and look out for **time apportionment**

Remember to add the **unwound** amount to the **provision** (Dr Finance costs, Cr Provisions) and state the **year end amount**, taking into account the unwound interest to state the **year end liability**

Indicate whether this is a **current or non-current liability** (generally it will be non-current if discounting has been applied because we are looking at an event some time into the future)

The **discount rate** to use will **normally be given** in the question – it should be a rate which reflects **current market assessments** of the time value of money and the **risks specific to the liability** (risk-adjusted rate) or the entity could use a risk-free rate and adjust the cash flows for risk – **risk must not be double-counted**

Onerous contracts (see also page 135)

If future benefits are expected to be less than unavoidable costs the contract is onerous

Excess unavoidable costs should be provided for at the time a contract becomes onerous

Restructuring costs

A constructive obligation arises where there has been a **detailed formal plan** regarding the employees affected and an announcement has been made to those who will be affected

Redundancy costs

Only provide for these if a formal announcement has been made

If the client has **mistakenly** created a provision then the correcting journal is likely to be

Dr Provisions (SFP)

Cr Staff expenses/Reorganisation costs (P&L)

Future costs

There must be a **past** obligating event for a **provision** to exist

Example: the costs of fitting smoke filters to comply with future legislation would **not** create a provision as there is no **past obligating** event but it would be correct to provide for the best estimate of fines for non-compliance which are likely to be imposed – in other words, whilst it would be economically and legally sensible for the company to install the filters, it is not actually obliged to do so whereas its actions have created a legal problem and it has thus become obligated to pay the relevant fines

Reimbursement from a third party

Normally this should be held **separately** from the provision

A reimbursement should only be recognised when it is **virtually certain** an amount will be received

Recognition and disclosure

A **full reconciliation** of **movements** in provisions should be presented – **detailed narrative explanation** should also be provided – the narrative should include an **estimate** of the financial amount in relation to contingent liabilities and assets as well as indications of uncertainties

Any **increase in the value of the discounted amount** arising from the **passage of time** or the **effect** of any **change in the discount rate** should be **disclosed**

Disclosure may be avoided if this would be **seriously prejudicial** to the position of the entity in dispute with other parties – however, this should only be employed in **extremely rare cases** – details of the **general** nature of the provision/contingent must still be provided, together with an explanation of **why** it has not been disclosed

Contingent liability – definition

A **past event** may lead to a liability in future but this will only be **confirmed** by the outcome of **some future event not wholly within the entity's control,** or **payment is not probable**, or the amount of payment cannot be **measured reliably**

A contingent liability is **disclosed** rather than recognised in the financial statements (unless the outflow of resources is thought to be **remote** in which case it is not even disclosed)

Regulatory Deferral Accounts

Applicability

IFRS 14 was issued in January 2014 and is effective for an entity's first annual IFRS financial statements for a period beginning on or after 1 January 2016

Applies to **first-time adopters of IFRS** that provide **goods or services to customers at a price or rate that is subject to rate regulation by the government** e.g. supply of gas or electricity

Need for IFRS 14

Given government **regulation** of prices, the prices charged to customers at a particular time do not necessarily **cover the costs** incurred by the supplier at that time – in this case the recovery of such costs is **deferred** and they are recognised though **future sales**

This leads to a **mismatch** – IFRS does not have specific requirements but practice is normally to recognise these amounts in the P&L as they arise

> However, local **GAAP** in **some countries** allows such activities to be recovered via a **separate regulatory deferral account** or **as part of the cost of a related asset** – IFRS 14 allows **first-time adopters of IFRS** to **continue** to recognise amounts related to rate regulation in accordance with their **previous GAAP** when they adopt IFRS via a **special exemption from IAS 8**

An entity **may change** its policy for regulatory deferral accounts **in accordance with IAS 8** but only if the change makes the financial statements **more relevant** and **reliable** to users

Presentation

The amounts of regulatory deferral account balances are **separately presented** in an entity's financial statements

Disclosures

Disclosures should be made to **enable users** to assess the **nature of, and risks associated with, the rate regulation that establishes the price(s) the entity can charge customers** for the goods or services it provides as well as the effects of rate regulation on the entity's financial statements

Related Party Transactions

Suggested mark allocation in an FR question (CR Q2): 3-4 marks

Signposts

Director **controls** one company and is in a position to **control or significantly influence a second company** which has some kind of **dealings with the first company** – this means that an entity is controlled by one of the key **management personnel** of another entity so the 2 entities are **related parties**

Contract terms not as standard e.g. a receivable with credit terms of 12 months

Look out for one of the entities being in **financial difficulties** – consideration should then be given to making an allowance for the debt and this would need to be **disclosed**

Definitions

A **person or close member of that person's family** is related to a reporting entity if that person

> has control or joint control over the reporting entity
>
> has significant influence over the reporting entity or
>
> is a **member of the key management personnel of the reporting entity** or of a parent of the reporting entity*

An **entity is related to a reporting entity** if

> the entity and reporting entity are members of the same group
>
> one entity is an associate or joint venture of the other entity
>
> both entities are joint ventures of the same third party
>
> one entity is a joint venture of a third entity and the other entity is an associate of the third entity
>
> the entity is a post-employment benefit plan for the benefit of employees of either the reporting entity or of an entity related to the reporting entity
>
> the entity is controlled or jointly controlled by a person identified under the first set of rules above (rules relating to a person or close member of that person's family)*
>
> a person with control or joint control over the reporting entity has significant influence over the entity or is a member of the key management personnel of the entity or of a parent of the entity

*Notice how these rules **interact**: a member of the key management personnel of the reporting entity is a related party of that entity and IAS 24 then says that if that individual controls another entity then that entity becomes a related party of the reporting entity (being a member of key management personnel whilst controlling another entity creates a **link** here)

Close members of the family of a person include that person's children and spouse or domestic partner, children of that person's spouse or domestic partner and dependants of that person or that person's spouse or domestic partner

Key management personnel

A member of **key management** of an entity is a **related party of that entity** – this includes Non-Executive Directors

Therefore the sale of company property to a marketing director (for example) would be a related party transaction

Not related parties

Two entities **just because** they have a director or member of key management personnel **in common** or **just because** a member of the key management personnel of one entity has significant influence over the other entity (it is, however, necessary to consider how that director would affect both parties)

Two venturers simply because they share joint control over a joint venture

Providers of finance, trade unions, public utilities and government departments that do not control, jointly control or significantly influence the reporting entity simply by virtue of their normal dealings with an entity

A customer, supplier, distributor etc who transacts a significant volume of business with the entity – there may be some economic dependence here but that is not sufficient to create a related party situation

Treatment

The existence of any relevant balances should be **disclosed** in the notes to the financial statements – **full disclosures** should be made **even if transactions took place on an arm's-length basis**

The fact that the transactions took place on an arm's-length basis may be disclosed but only if such terms can be **substantiated**

There should be disclosure of

> the **nature** of the relationship

> the **amount** of the transactions

> the **amount** of any **balances** outstanding at year-end

> any **provision** against outstanding balances and the expense recognised for bad and doubtful debts due from related parties

> any special terms and conditions attached to the balance

Note that there is no requirement to identify related parties by **name**

Transactions in relation to those balances should also be **disclosed** – for example, if there is a write-off of a loan to a director

It may be worth noting that the tax implications of such a transaction should also be considered, especially if it involves a foreign jurisdiction

Note that being **immaterial** is **not** an excuse to fail to disclose a related party transaction – the nature of related party transactions is that they are material by **nature**, rather than by **value**

Group scenarios

RPTs and outstanding balances with other entities in a group **are disclosed** in an **individual** entity's financial statements – these balances will be eliminated on consolidation in the financial statements of the **group** and are **not disclosed**

Research & Development

Suggested mark allocation in an FR question (CR Q2): 5-6 marks

Research phase (expense)

Treat as an **expense** as incurred – in this period there is **insufficient evidence** that the expenditure will generate **future** economic **benefits**

Investigation work will count as an **expense**

Development phase (capitalise)

Must meet strict criteria

> **technical feasibility** of completing the asset
>
> **intention** to complete the asset
>
> **ability** to use the asset
>
> demonstration of the **commercial viability** of the asset
>
> availability of **adequate resources**
>
> reliable measurement of expenditure

Tip – it takes time to write all of these criteria out – there will **be few or no marks simply for copying out** so try to **pick the criteria which help you show some knowledge of the exam scenario** and **start** with these (see our discussion of inline definition on page 6)

Capitalise from the date that all the criteria are met

Amortisation should **start** when the asset is **available for use** – note that this may be later than the time when the item is advertised/promoted/marketed: it must be available to be **used**

> If there is a gap between such dates, consider whether an **impairment review** is needed to ensure that the recoverable amount is not less than the carrying amount

Items not to capitalise (even after the criteria have been met)

Launch activities – such activities do not involve design, construction or testing and so should be expensed when incurred

Possible deferred revenue?

If payment has been made for some form of development to be delivered to the customer and the asset has not yet become ready to use, any payments already made by the customer will effectively be deposits as risks and rewards have not been transferred

These amounts must not be recognised as revenue but instead must be held as deferred income as part of current liabilities (assuming that the item will be delivered in the next accounting period: if not then a non-current liability may be appropriate)

Revenue Recognition

Suggested mark allocation in an FR question (CR Q2): 4-5 marks

Treatment

Recognition of a discount on a package of goods and services

Where a **package** of goods and services are sold, the components the package should be **identified**, **measured** and **recognised** as if **sold separately**

The same discount percentage should be applied to **each component** unless specific discount rates are known – the discount is found by comparing the **FV with the sales price**

Revenue on the **goods** element should normally be **recognised in the P&L in the year as normal** assuming that the equipment was sold in the year and therefore the **risks and rewards of ownership were transferred**

Revenue on the **services** element should be accounted for based on the **stage of completion** – this will often be a **straight line basis** in the absence of other information

Example

A package with fair value of 250,000 is sold for 200,000 – the **FV** of the **goods** components is 200,000 and the **FV** of the **services** component is 50,000

Here the discount is 50 / 250 or 20%

The **goods** element is therefore treated as revenue of 80% x 200,000 or 160,000 – this is probably recognised in **one amount** during the year

The **services** element is therefore treated as revenue of 80% x 50,000 or 40,000 – this is probably recognised over time and on a **straight line basis** if there is no better information

Check – 160,000 + 40,000 = 200,000 so we have therefore correctly allocated the actual sales revenue of 200,000

Reminder – compare the total **accounting** amount recognised in the year on goods and services against the **cash** received to determine if there is any **overpayment** (liability for our entity) or **underpayment** (asset for our entity) by the client

Recognition of services revenue

In relation to services, revenue should be recognised only when

> the amount can be **measured reliably**

> **probable** economic **benefits** will flow to the entity

> the **stage of completion** at the SFP date can be **reliably measured**

If **no services** at all had been provided to the customer at the year-end then **no revenue** should be recognised

Impairment of a receivable – percentage risk of default does not matter

If it is stated that, for example, there is a 5% risk of default then this does not mean that 5% of revenue should be de-recognised or impaired – this also applies in the case of credit risk to a receivable

Note that it has been suggested that IAS 18 **could** be **amended** to take account of the **likelihood** of default – for example, if there is a 5% likelihood of default then only 95% of the revenue would be recognised. A proposal to include this approach was not accepted in the latest Exposure Draft on revenue recognition

Online sales

The **timing** of the **receipt of cash** does **not** determine the **timing of revenue recognition** – revenue should be recognised when risks and rewards pass

This will normally be at the time of **physical delivery**

Sale with interest-free credit

Revenue should be **split** into **2** elements: the **fair value of the goods sold** and **finance income**

Each element should then be accounted for **separately**

To find the fair value of the goods sold, **discount** the amount to be paid at a future date – apply a **discount rate** based on the **credit status of customers**

A receivable should be included in the financial statements reflecting the current value of the discounted amount i.e. the amount receivable in future and on which an interest-free incentive has been given

As always, remember to unwind the discount to create **finance income** – look out for time apportionment here

Example

Value of goods sold £520,000 with 2 years of interest-free credit

Incremental borrowing rate for the entity is 7% and 10% for customers

A 10% deposit is paid at the time of purchase

Revenue on the **deposit** can be recognised immediately without any discounting so £52,000 is recognised as revenue immediately

The remaining £468,000 is not payable for 2 years so to find the fair value apply a discount at **10%** (customers' rate) over 2 years – £468,000 / 1.1^2 is £386,777 which can be **recognised** as revenue **immediately**

Finance income can then be recognised by **unwinding** the £386,777 by 10% for the relevant number of **months** (look out **time apportionment**) – remember to **update** the **year-end receivable** by the amount of finance income for the year as this will **not** have been received in **cash** since the customer will not pay until the end of the interest-free period

Loyalty card schemes

These are more like services than a transfer of goods

Associated revenue should be spread over the time period in which the relevant discount can be claimed

Example

Customers pay £25 each for loyalty cards and can claim a 20% discount for 3 years from the date of purchase

At the year-end, 9,000 cards had been issued with an average of 30 unexpired months on each card

Solution

Amount paid from the cards is £25 x 9,000 or £225,000 but this **cannot** all be recognised as revenue **immediately** – therefore deferred revenue will be created

Amount to recognise **this year** is for the 6 months of usage that has occurred on average this year (36 months available at purchase of the card less the 30 months average unexpired amount), expressed as a proportion of total revenue so 6 / 36 x £225,000 or £37,500

Amount to recognise **next year** (current liability) will be 12 / 36 x £225,000 or £75,000

Therefore the remaining balance must be a non-current liability of £225,000 - £37,500 - £75,000 or £112,500 (check – we have recognised 6 months and 12 months in the first 2 periods above so there must be 18 / 36 remaining and 18 / 36 x £225,000 is £112,500)

If **further information** is provided as to the **actual pattern of use** of the loyalty cards then this information should be used instead to calculate how much revenue should be recognised

Future accounting periods – IFRS 15

Note: IFRS 15 is not mandatory until 2018 so IAS 11 and IAS 18 remain the primary examinable standards for Corporate Reporting but you may now be examined on the impact of IFRS 15 in future accounting periods

A five step model will be used: identify the contract, identify the separate performance obligations, determine the transaction price, allocate the transaction price to the performance obligations and recognise revenue as the performance obligation is satisfied

Key impacts of IFRS 15 (may be worth mentioning **briefly** in your answers)

revenue only recognised on the transfer of goods and services to the customer (will affect some long-term contracts accounted for under the stage of completion model)

separate performance obligations will be recognised for distinct goods and services (which may be considered incidental only under current rules)

probability-weighted estimates will be required of the consideration to be received so some revenue may be recognised now even if there is a contingency based on a future event customer's credit risk will be reflected in the measurement of revenue so there may be recognition of revenue now (rather than deferral until collection of the consideration) even if there is uncertainty as to collectability

transaction price will be allocated to the standalone selling price (affecting any current policies which defer revenue if a company does not have objective evidence of the selling price of a good or service to be provided)

contract acquisition costs are to be expensed (affecting companies that currently capitalise and then amortise such costs)

Rights Issue

Suggested mark allocation in an FR question (CR Q2): 4 marks

Explanation

A rights issue provides current shareholders with newly issued shares in proportion to their existing holdings at a discount to the market price

Given the discount, a rights issue is in effect a combination of an issue at full market value and a bonus issue

An adjustment factor is therefore calculated to allow for the bonus element

This fraction is defined as **current market price / TERP** (calculated as explained below)

Only apply this fraction to the period **before** the rights issue – after the rights issue has taken place there is no need to apply the fraction: just increase the **total number of shares** to allow for the rights issue

Calculation of the TERP adjustment factor

Essentially, you are finding the average price under the **rights issue** – this is composed of a certain number of shares at the **current** market price plus **additional** shares (actually often just 1 share) at the **price in the rights issue**

Find the total value of the existing shares at the market value plus the cost of the rights issue and divide this by the number of shares including the rights issue (so if the issue is 1 for 3 then divide by 4)

Then create a fraction based on the current market price / average price just calculated

Example

1 for 3 rights issue at 132p when the market price is 220p

Existing	3	220	660
Rights share	1	132	132
	4		792

TERP is 792 / 4 or 198p

TERP fraction is therefore 220 / 198

> Always have the **higher** figure (**existing market price**) on the **top** of the fraction

Tip – quoting of the rights issue – "new for old"

Make sure you get the numbers of shares the right way round – the order in which the figures are quoted is based on a "new for old" basis

Therefore, a "1 for 3" rights issue means you will receive 1 new share for every 3 old or existing shares that you already have

Sale and Finance Leaseback

Suggested mark allocation in an FR question (CR Q2): 6 marks

This is essentially a **financing** arrangement – the entity is **not really disposing** of the asset because it is immediately **leased back** under a finance lease under which the entity gradually **buys back the asset** – the entity has maintained the **risks and rewards** of ownership **throughout** this entire process so there is no real sale

However, any profit earned is **deferred** over the lease term so that the overall impact of depreciation on the P&L each year is an amount equal to the depreciation expense **before** the leaseback transaction

Treatment

Derecognise the carrying amount of the asset now sold

Recognise the sales proceeds

Calculate the profit on sale as proceeds less carrying amount and recognise it as **deferred income** over the lease term

Recognise the finance lease asset and the associated liability and measure them in the normal way (at the lower of FV and the PV of MLP)

Impairment

If the **carrying amount** exceeds **fair value** then the asset should be written down to FV **before** the sale and leaseback and the **loss** recognised as an **impairment loss**

Sale and Operating Leaseback

Suggested mark allocation in an FR question (CR Q2): 6 marks

Signposts

The leaseback is for a **small portion** of the **useful economic life** of the asset

Treatment

The substance of the transaction is that of a **sale** – the asset is **sold** by the entity, transferring the risks and rewards of ownership to the other entity, and when it is **immediately leased back** there is **no** transferring back of risks and rewards as using the item under an operating lease **does not mean** the entity is **repurchasing** it

A **profit or loss on disposal** should be recognised **immediately** – however, look out for the need to **defer** some of the gain if the **sale proceeds are above the FV** (as this would not happen in a standard transaction)

In this case, the **difference** between the **carrying amount and FV** (normal profit) is **recognised immediately** but the unexpected difference between the **proceeds and the FV** is **deferred** and amortised over the **period in which the asset is expected to be used** (normally this will be the length of the lease)

Note that the client has probably recognised the full difference between the **carrying amount and proceeds** as a gain – therefore you will need to **reverse out a portion** (difference between process and FV) and treat this as **deferred income** – then if time apportionment is required (likely) apply our suggested technique to split the deferred income into current and non-current elements

1. Calculate a full year of deferred income – current liability

2. Time apportion the above figure from step 1 as required – current year P&L income

3. The remaining balance (i.e. the total amount minus the figures from step 1 in step 2) must be the non-current liability

Tabular summary of rules

Sale price at fair value

	Carrying amount equal to FV	Carrying amount below FV	Carrying amount above FV
Profit	No profit	Recognise profit immediately	N/A
Loss	No loss	N/A	Recognise loss immediately

Sale price below fair value

	Carrying amount equal to FV	Carrying amount below FV	Carrying amount above FV
Profit	No profit	Recognise profit immediately	No profit (Note 1)
Loss not compensated for by future lease rentals below market rate	Recognise loss immediately	Recognise loss immediately	(Note 1)
Loss compensated for by future lease rentals below market rate	Defer and amortise loss	Defer and amortise loss	(Note 1)

Sale price above fair value

	Carrying amount equal to FV	Carrying amount below FV	Carrying amount above FV
Profit	Defer and amortise profit	Defer and amortise (Proceeds less fair value) Recognise immediately (FV less carrying amount)	Defer and amortise profit (Note 2)
Loss	No loss	No loss	(Note 1)

Note 1

Carrying amount must be written down to FV with an accompanying impairment loss before the sale and leaseback is accounted for

Note 2

Profit is the difference between FV and sale price because the carrying amount would have been written down to FV

Sale and Repurchase

Suggested mark allocation in an FR question (CR Q2): 3 marks

In this situation, an entity **sells** an asset but has the **right** to repurchase at a particular price at a **later date**

Legal title passes but the arrangement may in **substance** be a **loan** as the entity is receiving money now and will repay this later whilst maintaining ownership of the asset throughout the period

If the repurchase is at a price **below the current market price** then this adds weight to the conclusion that the sale is not a **genuine sale**

Treatment

Revenue should **not** be **recognised** as there is **no genuine sale**

Therefore **profit** should **not be recognised either** – the profit recognised was probably calculated as proceeds less carrying amount so this needs to be reversed

Set up a **loan account** equal to the **proceeds** and charge a **finance cost** based on the **applicable interest rate** (should be given in the question)

Update the **loan receivable** at the year-end for the **accrued interest** based on the loan value at the interest rate (look out for the **time apportionment**) – state the **year end loan balance** and indicate whether this is a **current** or **non-current** liability

Share-based payment – cash-settled

Suggested mark allocation in an FR question (CR Q2): 6 marks

A **cash-settled** share-based scheme makes a payment of **cash** to the employee based on the value of the entity's equity instruments – the employee does not receive any **shares** but rather the **cash value** of those shares – **make sure this is stated in your answer**

Treatment

Recognise an expense over the period that the related services are provided – for example, straight line over 3 years if the employee is required to work for 3 years before settlement of the incentive

The expense is based on the FV of the options – for a cash-settled scheme (and not for an equity-settled scheme) you should take into account changes in the FV of the options each year

> To find this year's charge, use the latest available FV but then look back to see what was already charged – do not go back and change any prior figures but deduct amounts already recognised as an expense or equity when calculating this year's charge

Remember to use a spreading fraction such as 1/3 in year 1 of a 3 year scheme, 2/3 in year 2 of a 3 year scheme, and so on – but then also allow for the amounts recognised in the prior year

Debit employment expenses and Credit a liability account (probably non-current but check) with the expense for the year

> Again, with a cash settled scheme you use the latest available FV to find the cumulative expense and cumulative credit to liabilities but to find this year's debits and credits you need to deduct off any amounts already recognised

(This final stage is not necessary with an equity-settled scheme because the FV never changes once the scheme starts so you can just use the same amounts every year if there is no change in the expected number of employees who will exercise their options.)

Typical cash-settled working

400 employees x 100 options per employee x £16 FV this year x 1/3 for year 1 of a 3 year scheme

380 employees x 100 options per employee x £14 FV this year x 2/3 for year 2 of a 3 year scheme

> Expense and liability found by calculating based on a 2/3 fraction and then deducting previously recognised amounts (as per year 1 calculation, in this case)

475 employees x 100 options per employee x £17 FV this year x 3/3 for year 3 of a 3 year scheme

> Expense and liability found by calculating based on a 3/3 fraction and then deducting previously recognised amounts (as per year 1 and 2 calculations, in this case)

Remember that the 2/3 and 3/3 fractions will find the **total** expense and **total** liability of the scheme – deduct any previously recognised amounts to find this year's charge/liability entry

Also always look out for time-apportionment!

See also our section on Share Appreciation Rights starting on page 170.

Share-based payment – equity-settled

Suggested mark allocation in an FR question (CR Q2): 6 marks

The **fair value** of the options at the grant date should be treated as an **expense** in the P&L and **spread** over the vesting period, from the grant date until the date the scheme conditions vest

Only allocate an **expense** based on the **number of employees expected to be in position** at the date the options **vest** i.e. on the **final day** of the scheme

Make sure you **state in your answer** why the scheme is treated as equity-settled – this is because the employee receives **shares** or **equity**

Typical calculation for an equity-settled scheme (assuming some time apportionment)

Number of options per employee x employees who will qualify x FV at grant date x spreading fraction (e.g. 1/3 to spread over 3 years) x time apportionment (e.g. 9/12)

This amount should be charged to the **P&L** with a corresponding **credit in the SFP to equity** – IFRS 2 does not state **where** in equity this entry should arise but many companies add it to **retained earnings**

Dr Employee expenses (P&L)

Cr Retained earnings (SFP)

If the number of employees expected to qualify does not change then the charge will be the same for all years of the scheme (as changes in the FV of the options are not taken into account, unlike with a cash-settled scheme)

Market-based scheme conditions – ignore

Any condition relating to changes in the entity's **share price** is termed a "**market-based** condition"

This type of condition is completely **ignored** in an equity settled scheme – the **possibility of changes** in the share price and the consequent impact on the fair value of the share option is already built into the **initial fair value** of the option

If the shares or share options **do not ultimately vest** because the condition is not met, any amount **already recognised** in the financial statements **will remain** and **will not be adjusted**

Non-market-based scheme conditions – consider

Any condition which does **not** relate to changes in the entity's **share price** is termed a "non-market-based condition"

This kind of condition **is** taken into account in the case of an equity-settled scheme

There will almost always be **one** such condition i.e. that the employee must **continue to work for the entity at the vesting date**

If there are other such conditions, **only the number of shares or share options expected to vest** will be accounted for, taking into account **whether** the **condition** is **likely** to be met – on the vesting date, the entity should **revise** the **estimate** based on the number of shares or share options that **do actually vest** – this could mean **cancelling out** some prior year figures

Combination of market- and non-market-based conditions

If a scheme has **both** types of condition attached, the **market conditions should be ignored as normal** so provided that **all** other **non-market** vesting conditions are satisfied then an expense and related credit to equity should be recognised

In other words, the **non-market**-based conditions are the conditions which matter

The amounts recognised each year will therefore have **no connection to movements in the entity's share price**

Modification or repricing of share options e.g. a change in the exercise price

Continue to recognise the original fair value in the normal way – recognise any **increase** in fair value at the modification date by **spreading** this over the **period between the modification date and vesting date**

If the modification occurs **after** the vesting date, the additional fair value is recognised **immediately unless there is an additional service period**, in which case the difference is **spread** over this period

Cancellations and settlements

Immediately charge any remaining fair value not already recognised in profit or loss – the cancellation or settlement therefore **accelerates** the expense and **prevents the entity avoiding it**

If an amount is paid to employees on settlement, this is treated as a **buyback of shares** and should be recognised as a **deduction from equity** – if the amount is in **excess of the fair value** of the equity instruments granted, the **excess** should be **recognised immediately in profit or loss**

Variable vesting date

The calculation should be based on the **best estimate** of when vesting will occur

Vested options not exercised

This is the choice of the **holder** of the equity instruments as an investor – therefore there is **no impact** on the **financial statements** of the **entity**

IFRS 2 does permit a transfer to be made **between reserves** to avoid an amount remaining in a separate equity reserve where no equity instrument will be issued

Deferred tax

In many jurisdictions, a tax allowable expense is available at the **date of exercise**, measured on the basis of the option's **intrinsic value** on that date i.e. the difference between **market price** of a share and the **exercise price** under the share option scheme

The market price of a share at exercise cannot be known with certainty before exercise so in the deferred tax calculations which are needed in the accounting periods before exercise an **estimate** is made based on **assuming that the share price at the end of the current accounting period will also be the share price on the exercise date** – this is the best estimate possible

The total **difference** between the exercise price and assumed future share price (**intrinsic value**) is then **spread** over time to match with the accounting expense recognised under IFRS 2 – an amount **up to the value of the accounting expense** is recognised as a deferred tax asset (SFP) and deferred tax credit (P&L) as the entity benefits from future tax deductibility – any **excess** deferred tax benefit above the accounting expense is recognised directly in **equity**

See also our Deferred tax section starting on page 38

Possible methods to determine the fair value of an equity settled share option

Black-Scholes model

Binomial model

Monty Carlo simulation

Share-based payment schemes with a choice of settlement (equity-settled or cash-settled)

Counterparty has the choice over how the scheme is settled

Apply **split accounting** – the entity has issued an instrument with a **debt** component insofar as the recipient may demand **cash** and an **equity** component so far as the recipient may demand settlement in **equity** instruments

First measure the **fair value** of the **debt** component – the **equity** component will then be a **residual** or **balancing** amount.

Example

A scheme allows the counterparty to choose between 10,000 shares (shares option) or cash to the value of 9,000 shares (cash option) on the grant date. The market price of the entity's shares on the grant date is £20 and the fair value of a share option on the grant date is £19.

In this case, the fair value of the cash route is 9,000 x £20 market price or £180,000 whilst the fair value of the share route is 10,000 x £19 or £190,000.

Therefore the fair value of the debt element is £180,000 (cash route) and the balancing fair value of the equity component under split accounting is £10,000 (£190,000 - £180,000).

Finally, treat the **debt** element like a **cash-settled scheme** with the usual **spreading** approach and **taking into account** changes in fair value each year – treat the **equity** element like an **equity-settled scheme** with the **usual spreading approach** and **not taking into account** changes in fair value each year

Entity has the choice over how the scheme is settled

Treat as a **cash-settled** scheme to the extent it has a **present obligation** to deliver **cash** e.g. the entity is **prohibited** from issuing **shares** or has a **stated policy** or **past practice** of issuing **cash** rather than **shares**

If **no present obligation** to deliver **cash** exists, the entity should treat the transaction as a purely **equity-settled** transaction – if this equity treatment is applied but **cash is actually paid on settlement**, the cash should be treated as a **repurchase** of the **equity instrument** by a **deduction against equity**

Share-based payment – payment for goods and services

Suggested mark allocation in an FR question (CR Q2): 3 marks

Note – this scenario relates to a situation where a **supplier** is paid in the form of the entity's own shares rather than with cash or via a payable – it does not relate to a scenario involving an **employee**

Treatment

State that the transaction is within the scope of IFRS 2

State that it is an "equity settled" transaction because the entity has received goods in exchange for an issue of shares

This type of transaction should be measured at the **fair value of the goods and services received** and **not** at the value of the **shares** themselves

> Therefore look out for an examiner trick – **the fair value of the entity's shares does not matter** – it is the **fair value of the goods and services** which is used

The journal entries should be

Dr Expenses (e.g. consultancy costs, purchases)

Cr Equity

There should not be recognition of any payable here – the credit entry should be to Equity as the entity will not be paying cash but rather shares or **equity**

Increase share capital by the nominal value of shares and place any excess into Share premium

Example – the entity obtains services with a fair value of 70,000 in exchange for shares with a nominal value of 20,000

Debit	Expenses	70,000
Credit	Share capital	20,000
Credit	Share premium (balance)	50,000

Example

A consultant provide services with a FV of 50,000 but is paid in the form of the entity shares which are worth 75,000 – use the figure of 50,000 to recognise this transaction

Tip – again, use the **FV** of the **goods and services** – ignore the FV of the **shares** offered in return

Share-based payment – Share Appreciation Rights

Suggested mark allocation in an FR question (CR Q2): 3 marks

This kind of instrument is deemed to be cash-settled as there is no issue of shares (therefore not equity-settled)

The treatment is similar to a cash-settled scheme i.e. **do** consider **updates in FV** at each year end

Non-market conditions

These conditions should be taken into account

Continued employment through to the vesting date will almost certainly be a condition of the scheme and is a non-market-based condition which must be considered

Treatment

Liability created in the SFP and an **expense** is recognised in the P&L

FV is re-measured each reporting date, taking into account the number of employees who are expected to qualify

Share-based payment – share options

Suggested mark allocation in an FR question (CR Q2): 6 marks

See also page 164 for cash-settled schemes and page 165 for equity-settled schemes.

Treatment

Identify **whether cash-settled** or **equity-settled** and briefly **explain** the **reasons** for your choice of classification

Cash-settled

Remember to state why you are treating the scheme as cash-settled

Recognise an expense over the period that the related services are provided – for example, straight line over 3 years if the employee is required to work for 3 years before settlement of the incentive

The expense is based on the FV of the options – for a cash-settled scheme (and not for an equity-settled scheme) you should take into account changes in the FV of the options each year

> To find this year's charge, use the latest available FV but then look back to see what was already charged – do not go back and change any prior figures but **deduct amounts already recognised** as an expense or liability when calculating this year's charge

Remember to use a spreading fraction such as 1/3 in year 1 of a 3 year scheme, 2/3 in year 2 of a 3 year scheme, and so on – but then also allow for the amounts recognised in the prior year

Debit employment expenses and Credit a liability account (probably non-current but check) with the expense for the year

> Again, with a **cash settled** scheme you use the **latest available FV** to find the cumulative expense and cumulative credit to liabilities but to find this year's debits and credits you need to deduct off any amounts already recognised

(This final stage is not necessary with an equity-settled scheme because the FV never changes once the scheme starts so you can just use the same amounts every year.)

Equity-settled

Remember to state why you are treating the scheme as equity-settled

Record an annual expense in profit or loss, spread over the vesting period with a corresponding annual increase in equity – IFRS 2 does not state where in equity the Credit arises: many companies add it to retained earnings

Measure each option at the FV at the grant date

Remove the year end estimate of total leavers over the whole vesting period from the calculation of the expense – we are only interested in allowing for the staff who are estimated to be in place at the time that the share options can be exercised

Market-based vesting criteria (based on changes in the share price) should not be considered each year as the estimates of FV will already have taken these movements into account in the valuation model – therefore it does not matter whether the target is or is not met at the year end

Non-market-based vesting criteria (such as a profit target or margin target) should be considered at each year end to determine if vesting is probable – use the existing information as the best estimate of the likely scenario at the vesting date

Example first year calculation – remember to replace the figures with your information!

500 employees x 60% expected to remain x 100 options per employee x £3 FV x 1/5 vested

You do not need to write the words "employees", "expected to remain", "options per employee", "FV" or "vested" when writing the calculation into your answer – we have only included these for tutorial purposes

If you are looking at the second or later year, you would use a fraction such as 2/5, 3/5 and so on at the end of the calculation – compare this with all previous amounts already expensed in previous years to determine the net expense and incremental updating net credit to equity for the year you are looking at

| See also | Share-based payment – cash-settled | p164 |
| | Share-based payment – equity-settled | p165 |

Social and environmental reporting

Companies Act 2006 requires **quoted** companies to include information on **environmental**, **employment** and **social** issues as part of the business review contained in the Directors' Report

From 1 October 2013, **quoted** companies must also report on **greenhouse gas emissions** in their Directors' Report

Unquoted companies are **encouraged** to provide this information **voluntarily** as **best practice**

Auditor considerations

It is possible that the audit firm has not been involved in assurance regarding social and environmental report before

The firm should ensure that it has **relevant expertise and resources** to complete the assignment

An **engagement letter** should be used to **clarify responsibilities** as these are **not defined by law**

It is **permissible** to provide **other services** (such as assurance over social and environmental reporting) under ethical guidance for auditors but the firm should consider the **level of the fee** to be received and ensure that the firm is **not economically dependent** on the client

The **social and environmental report** is expected to be included in the **same document** that contains the **audited financial statements**

If any of the **proposed assertions** are found to be **inconsistent** with the audited financial statements and management **refuses** to resolve the issue we would need to consider what impact this would have on the **auditor's report** and **whether** we should **continue the audit engagement**

Staff bonuses

Suggested mark allocation in an FR question (CR Q2): 2 marks

Constructive obligations

Past practice or an **announcement** will create a **constructive obligation** – this is treated as a **provision** as it is an **obligation** relating to a **past event**

Calculate the provision based on the number of employees expected to claim the bonus, using the scheme criteria e.g. 50 employees x 5% bonus rate x salaries

Dr Staff expenses (P&L)

Cr Provisions (SFP)

Employer's **National Insurance** at 13.8% would also be due on a bonus – remember that as the bonus (plus employer's National Insurance) would be tax deductible a tax saving would also be possible (e.g. actual cost would be **1 - tax rate** times the pre-tax cost) – CR is **not** a **tax exam** so mention these 2 points very **briefly**

The bonus should only be recognised when there is a **constructive** or **legal** obligation to make payment

This could relate to **conditions** in a related **contract** or could be based on **past practice**

Remember to look out for **time apportionment**

Treasury shares

Suggested mark allocation in an FR question (CR Q2): 2 marks

Tip – this question is not worth many marks so must be done **quickly** but at the same time it is **quite easy to score all the marks available** as the answer never varies from our points noted below

Points to mention

Equity instruments reacquired are known as Treasury shares

These are deducted from equity and shown as a separate (negative) reserve

Original share capital and share premium amounts remain unchanged

No gain or loss should be recognised on the issue, sale, purchase or cancellation of Treasury shares

Notes

Notes

Notes

Notes

Notes

Notes

Feedback

We hope that you found this book useful – we can only improve our learning materials and tuition services with your feedback so please feel free to get in touch at **getqualified@acasimplified.com**.

www.acasimplified.com

Printed in Great Britain
by Amazon